DINOSAUR
ACTIVITY BOOK

ScribbleKids Press

Connect with us!

Visit us online at
www.ScribbleKidsPress.com

Email: scribblekidspress@gmail.com

Copyright © 2023 ScribbleKids Press LLC

ISBN-13: 978-1-960195-09-8

All rights reserved. No part of this publication may be reproduced, distributed, or transmitted in any form or by any means, including photocopying, recording, or other electronic or mechanical methods, without the prior written permission of the publisher, except in the case of brief quotations embodied in critical reviews and certain other noncommercial uses permitted by copyright law.

This book belongs to

Hi friend!

My name is Cera and I am so glad that you are here! I need your help with these activities. Do you think you can show me how to do each one? Don't worry, we will be meeting many of my friends along the way who will help us complete our adventure!

Let's get started!

TRACE ME

Let's begin with some line tracing. Can you show me how to draw the horizontal, vertical and diagonal lines below?

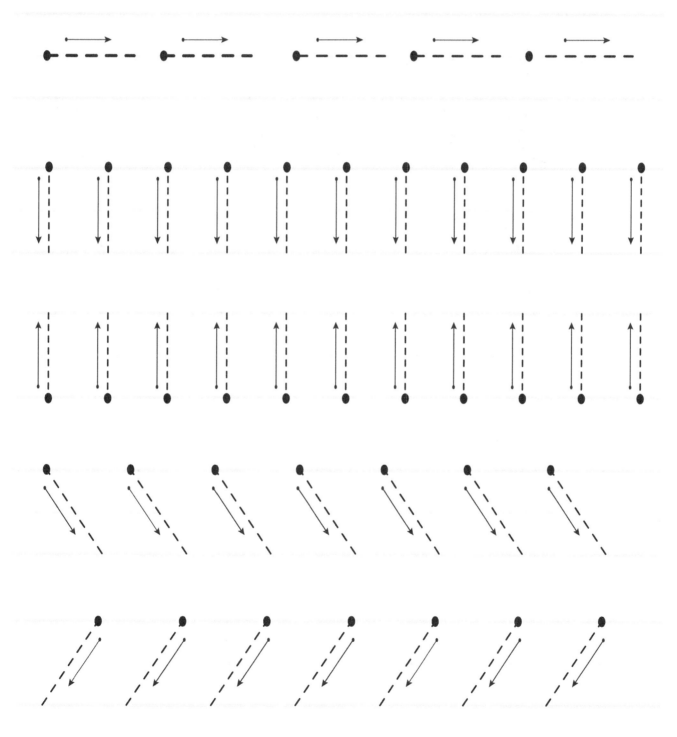

TRACE ME

Ooo! Look! Swirls and bumps! Can you show me how you do these?

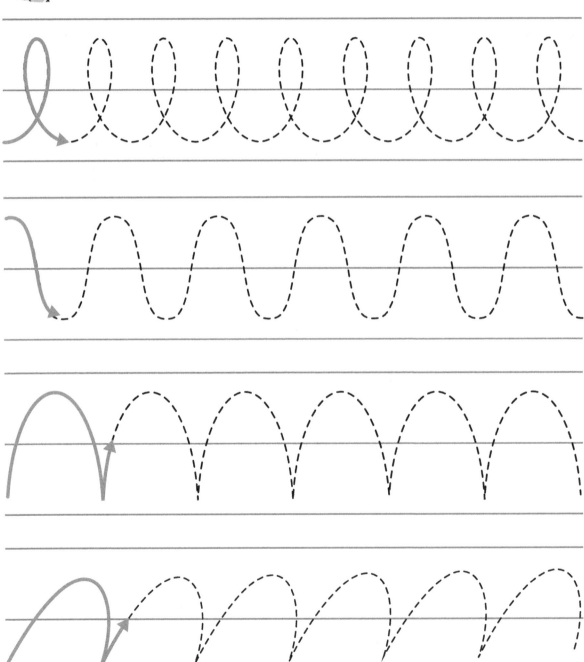

TRACE ME

These look like so much fun! Up and down we go! There's even a spiral! Don't get dizzy...

Hi friend!

Can you believe that 52 dinosaurs are here to help us with the next part! They are looking forward to meeting you.

Let's keep going! You're doing great!

TRACE ME

Before Tank and Pat join us, let's do a fun review of our ABC's! Can you complete the following dinosaur going from A-Z?

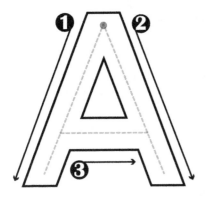

Ankylosaurus
(Ang-kuh-low-saw-ruhs)

Trace and write **A**. Start at the dot ●

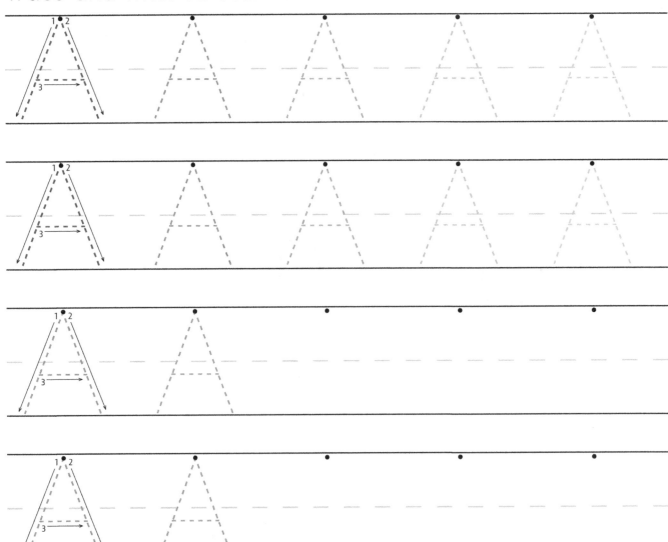

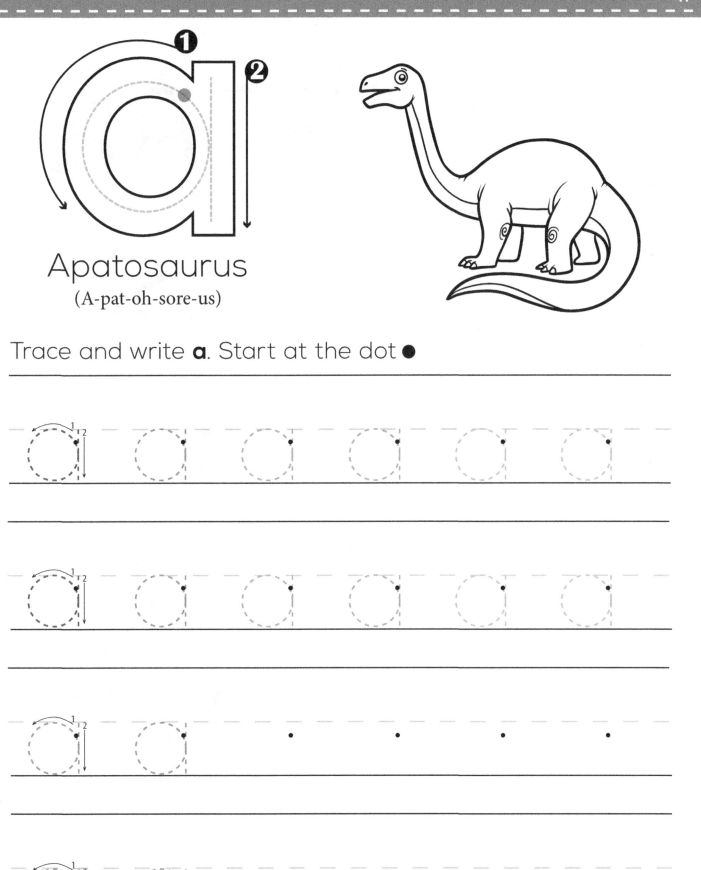

Find the circles with the uppercase letter **A** and color them **red**. Find lowercase letter **a** and color them **brown**.

Aa

PUZZLE

Let's do a puzzle!

Find your way from the **start** to the **finish**, following the lowercase letter **a**.

Start

a	t	z	f	j	i	p	t	b	i	n	r
	a	a	a	a	a	a	w	z	x	t	s
	v	y	i	l	z	a	u	y	j	p	q
x	c	k	p	w	p	k	y	a	a	f	o	v
u	z	n	o	u	h	o	x	e	v	a	g	l	u
t	b	m	q	r	a	a	a	a	a	a	e	j	w
a	a	a	a	a	a	n	c	d	q	c	d	m	k
a	e	l	r	q	v	m	b	h	o	h	a
a	a	a	a	a	a	a	a	a	a	a
w	y	d	s	s	x	g	f	g	r	s

Finish

B

Brachiosaurus
(brae-kee-uh-saw-ruhs)

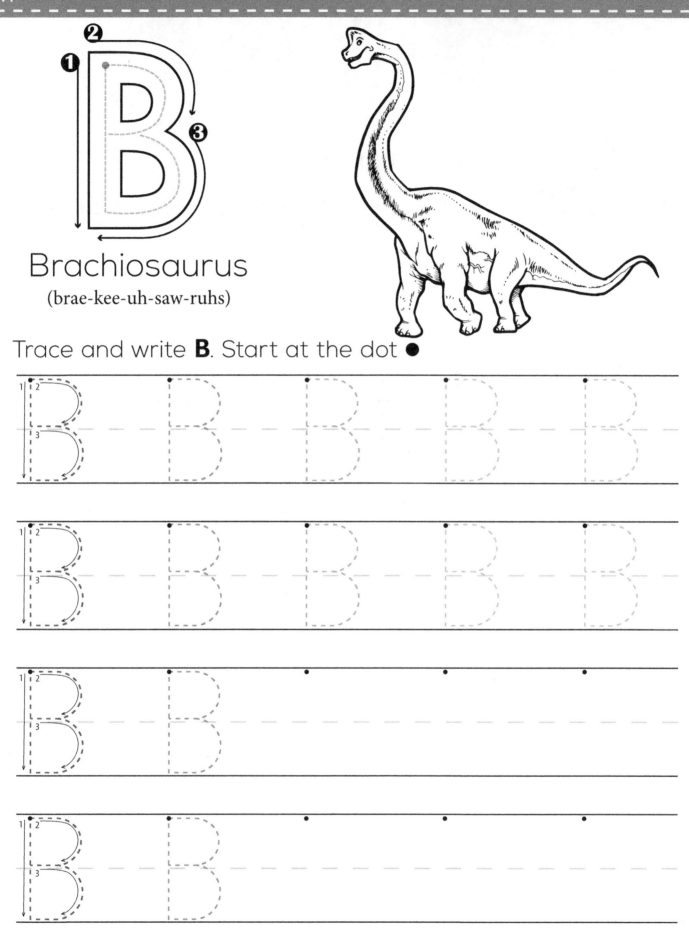

Trace and write **B**. Start at the dot ●

Brontosaurus
(Bron-toe-sor-us)

Trace and write b. Start at the dot ●

Find the circles with the uppercase letter **B** and color them **blue**. Find lowercase letter **b** and color them **black**.

Bb

D b A
B B b C
A c a b
b a B
d B D

COLOR ME

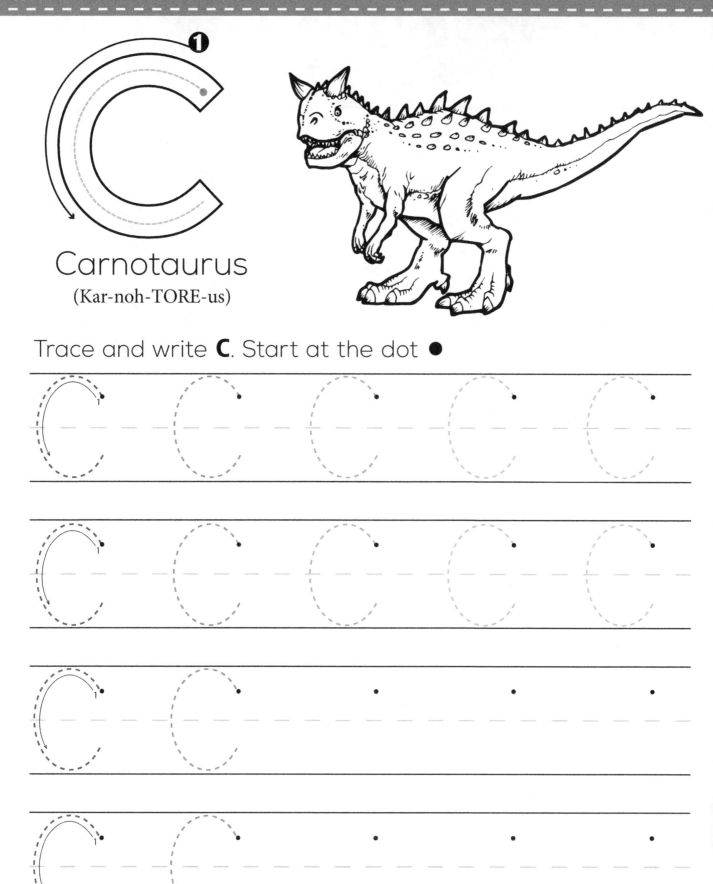

Carnotaurus
(Kar-noh-TORE-us)

Trace and write **C**. Start at the dot ●

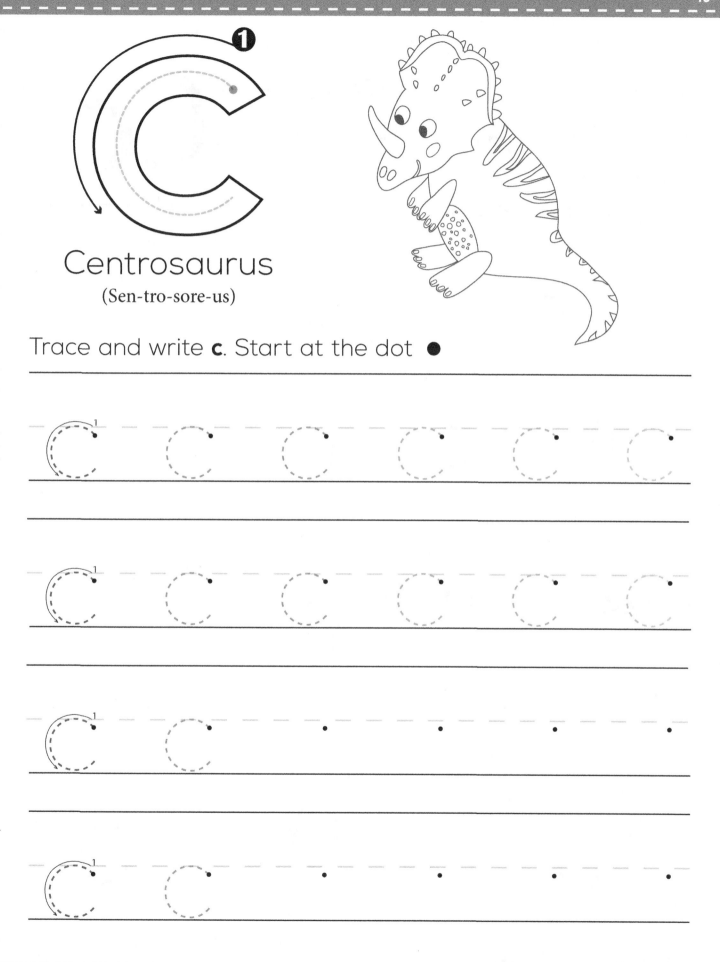

Find the circles with the uppercase letter **C** and color them **cyan**. Find lowercase letter **c** and color them **crimson**.

Cc

My friend drake really wants to be colored! Find and color the circles the following:

A: Orange **b:** Yellow
a: Green **C:** Purple
B: Blue **c:** Pink

PUZZLE

Can you help the Carnotaurus find her egg?

PUZZLE

Can you help? These dinosaurs need to find their nests. Trace the lines to find each one. Then write the letter in the box.

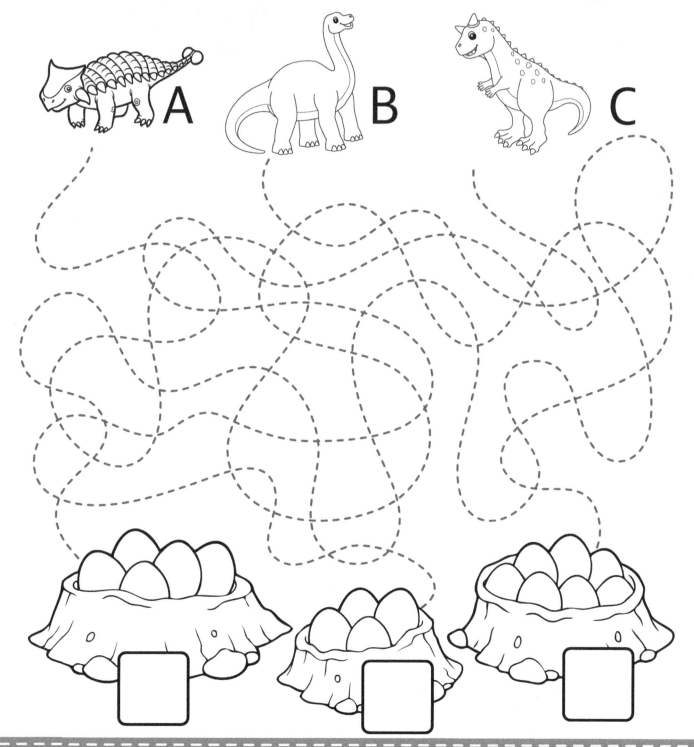

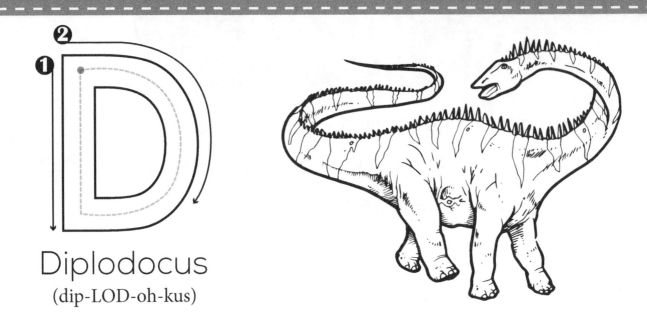

Diplodocus
(dip-LOD-oh-kus)

Trace and write **D**. Start at the dot ●

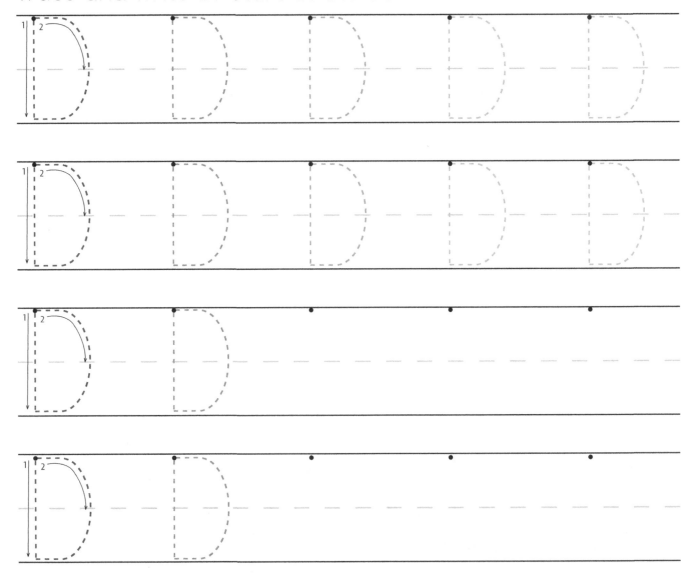

Deinonychus
(Die-non-e-cus)

Trace and write **d**. Start at the dot ●

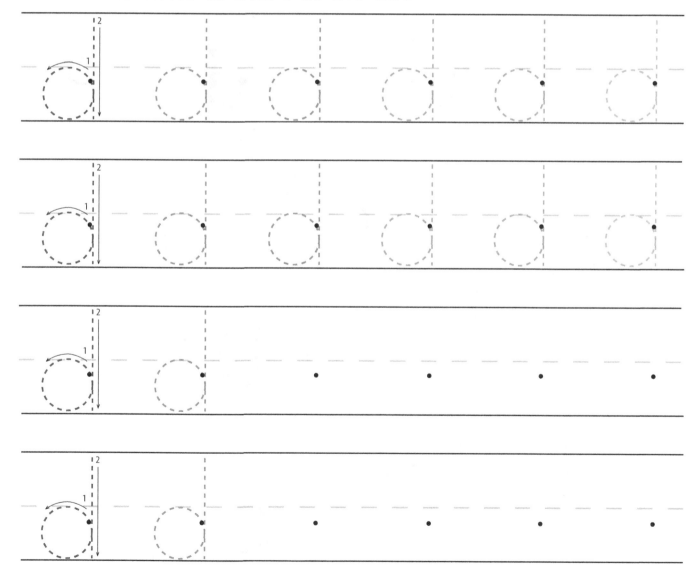

Find the circles with the uppercase letter **D** and color them **blue**. Find lowercase letter **d** and color them **orange**.

Dd

PUZZLE

Let's do a puzzle!

Find your way from the **start** to the **finish**, following the lowercase letter **d**.

Start

Finish

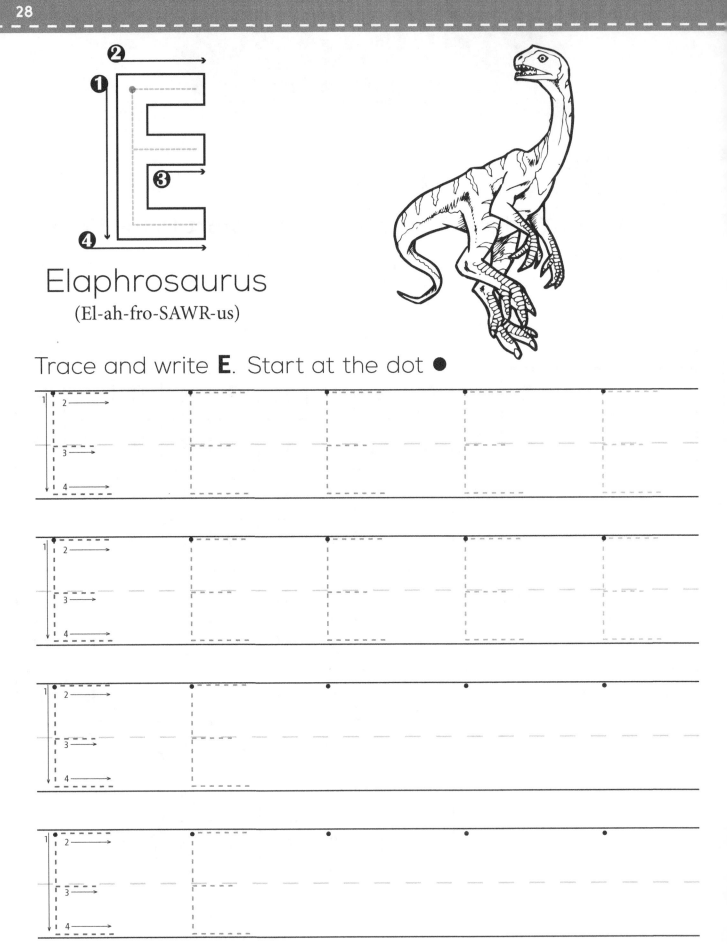

Elaphrosaurus
(El-ah-fro-SAWR-us)

Trace and write **E**. Start at the dot ●

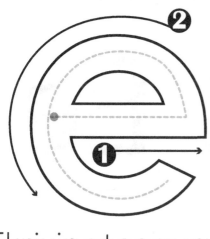

Ekrixinatosaurus
(Ek-riks-in-at-oh-sore-us)

Trace and write **e**. Start at the dot ●

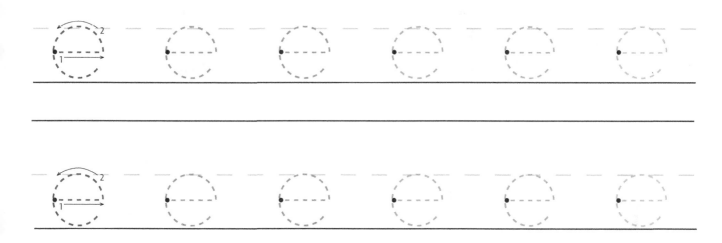
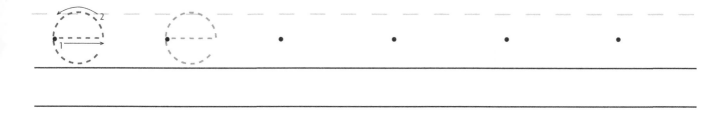

Find the circles with the uppercase letter **E** and color them **purple**. Find lowercase letter **e** and color them **yellow**.

Ee

PUZZLE

Oh no! The dinosaurs lost their shadows! Let's help them find the right ones. Draw a line from the left to the right when you find a match.

PUZZLE

Can you help me with each pattern? Write the letter in the empty box that's next to the image that continues the pattern.

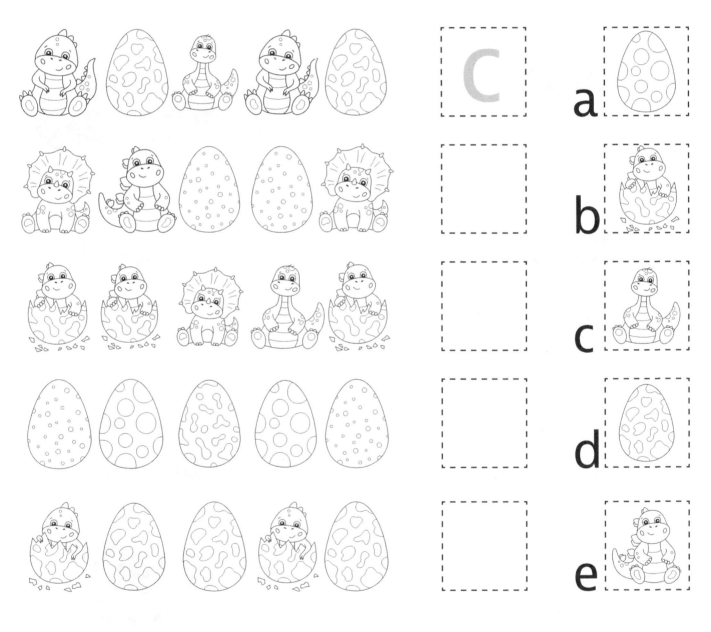

TRACE ME

These dinosaurs are going for a walk.
Can you help them by tracing the lines?

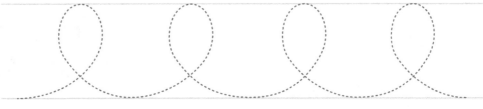

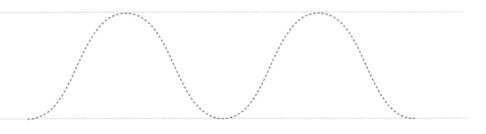

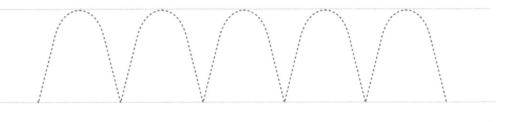

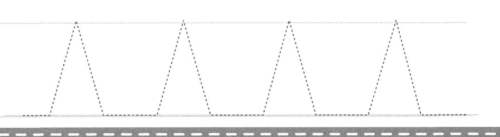

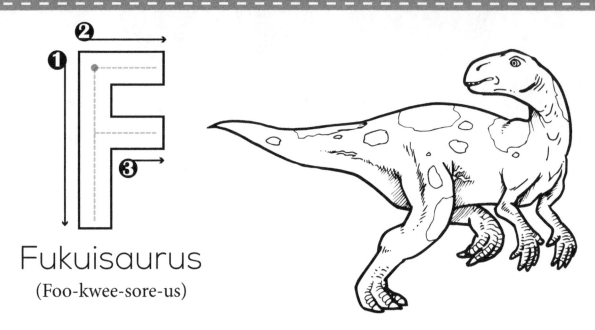

Fukuisaurus
(Foo-kwee-sore-us)

Trace and write **F**. Start at the dot ●

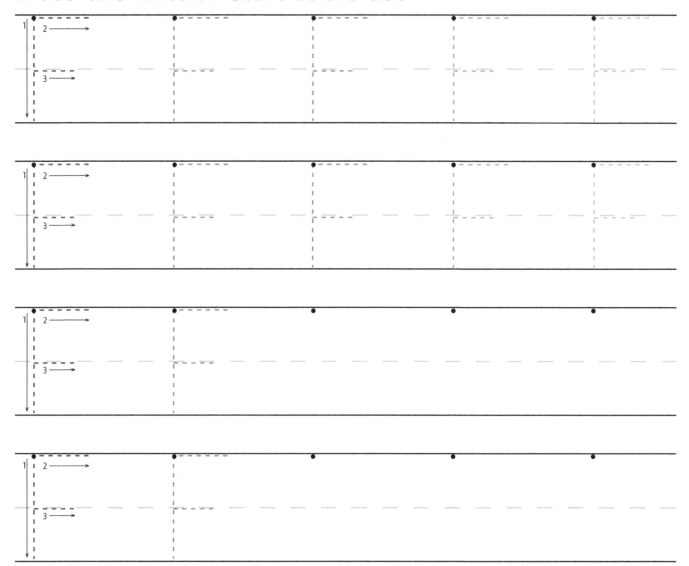

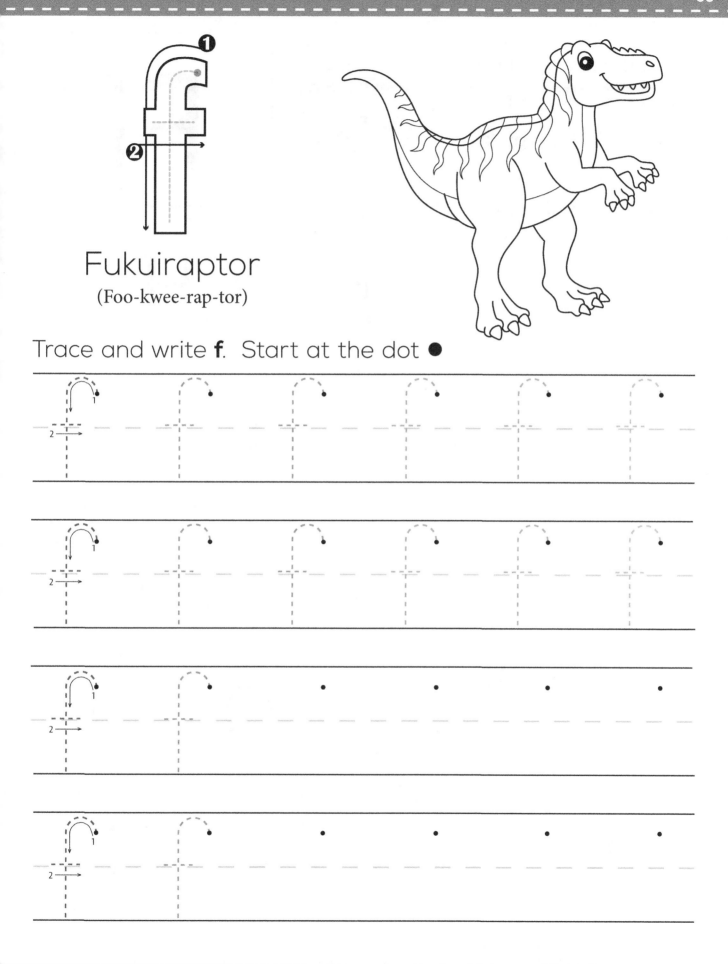

Find the circles with the uppercase letter **F** and color them **pink**. Find lowercase letter **f** and color them **grey**.

Ff

F f H
b B F f
E a D
E D f
F f c f
C

 Fu loves being the center of attention. He wants his picture drawn! Can you draw Fu so he can give the picture to his mom?

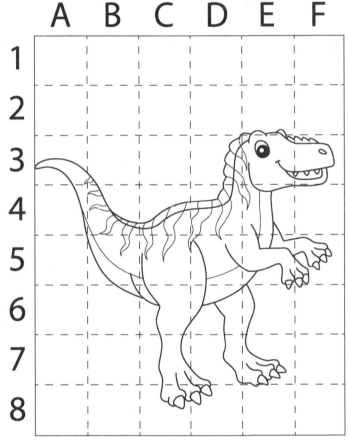

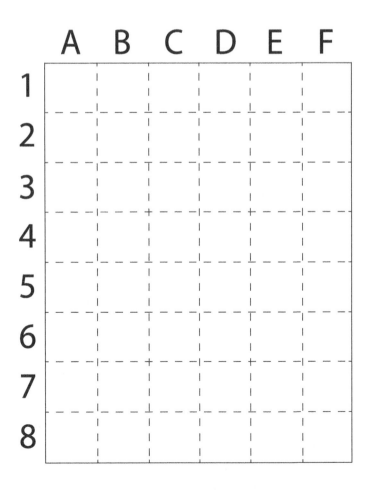

Garudimimus
(Gah-ru-di-mime-us)

Trace and write **G**. Start at the dot ●

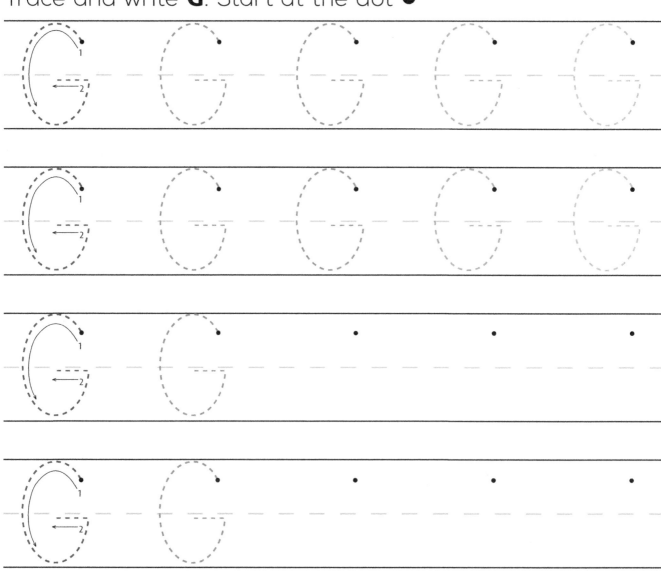

Gigantosaurus
(Gy-gant-o-sore-us)

Trace and write **g**. Start at the dot ●

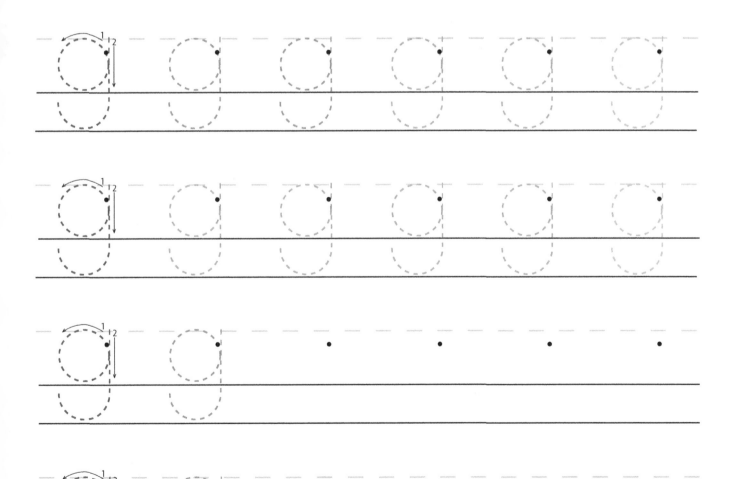

Find the circles with the uppercase letter **G** and color them **red**. Find lowercase letter **g** and color them **green**.

Gg

PUZZLE

Can you help Gigi find her friend Erik?

They want to play together!

Start

Finish

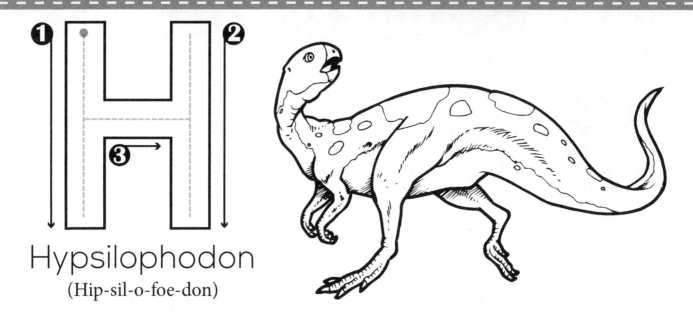

Hypsilophodon
(Hip-sil-o-foe-don)

Trace and write **H**. Start at the dot ●

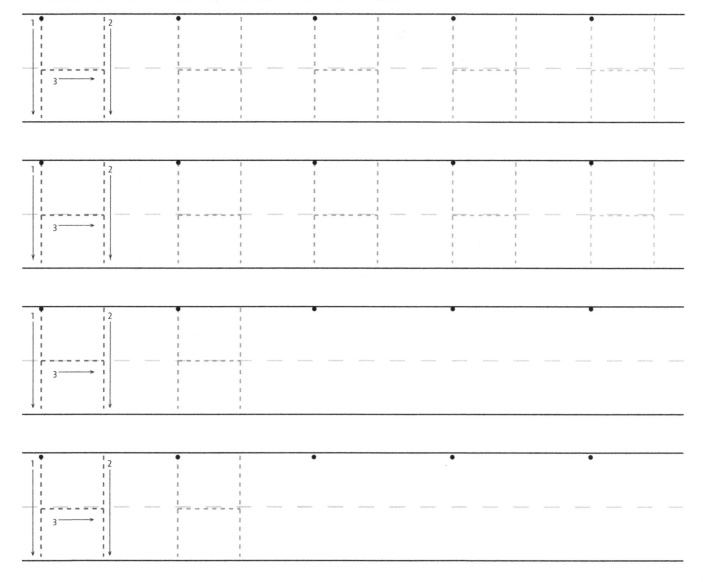

Hesperosaurus
(Hes-per-o-sore-us)

Trace and write **h**. Start at the dot ●

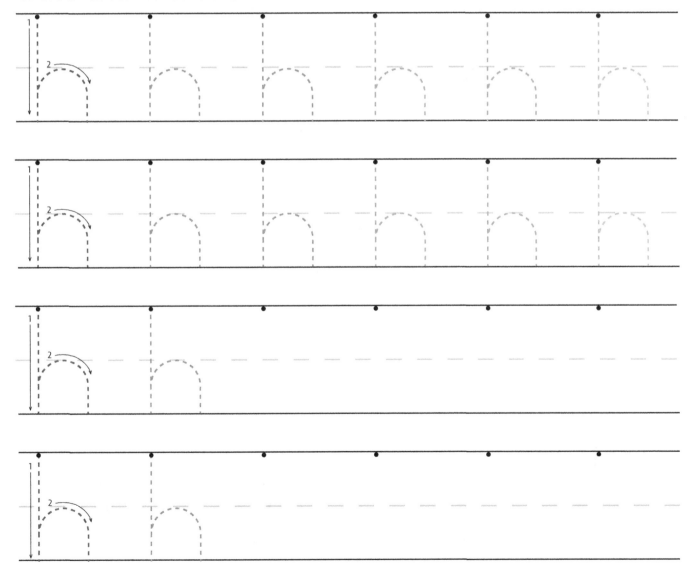

Find the circles with the uppercase letter **H** and color them **orange**. Find lowercase letter **h** and color them **brown**.

Hh

COLOR ME

My friend Perry would love to be colored. Can you help him?

E: Light red

F: Dark red

G: Yellow

H: Orange

I LOVE matching! Can you help me match the uppercase and lowercase letters?

A B C D

d c a b

E F G H

h g e f

 Let's do a quick review! Trace the letters below and say the sound each one makes.

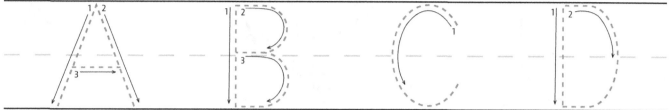

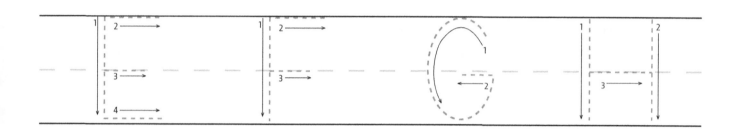

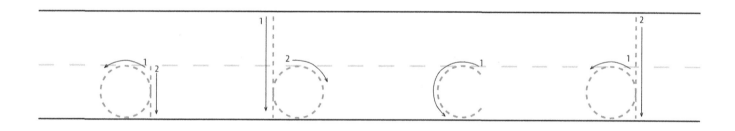

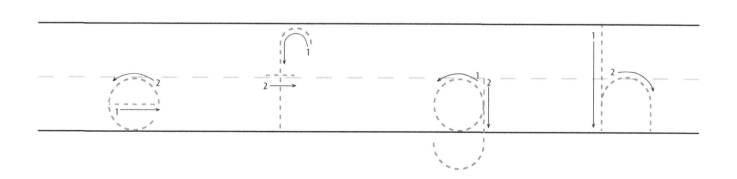

Iguanodon
(Ig-wah-no-don)

Trace and write I. Start at the dot ●

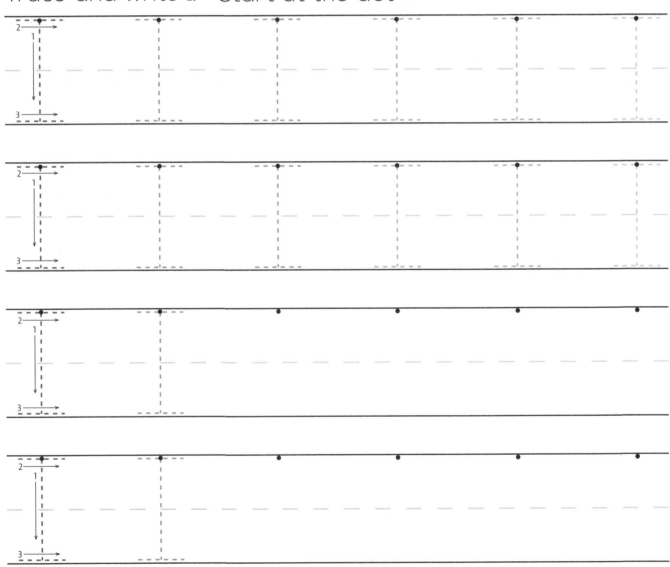

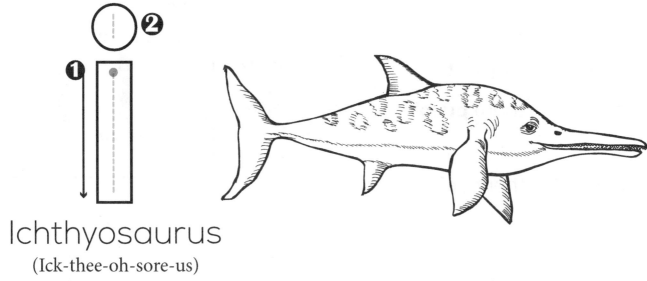

Ichthyosaurus
(Ick-thee-oh-sore-us)

Trace and write **i**. Start at the dot ▼

Find the circles with the uppercase letter **I** and color them **purple**. Find lowercase letter **i** and color them **yellow**.

Ii

Let's do a puzzle!

Find your way from the **start** to the **finish**, following the lowercase letter **i**.

Start

Finish

Juravenator
(Jooh-ah-ven-ah-tor)

Trace and write **J**. Start at the dot ●

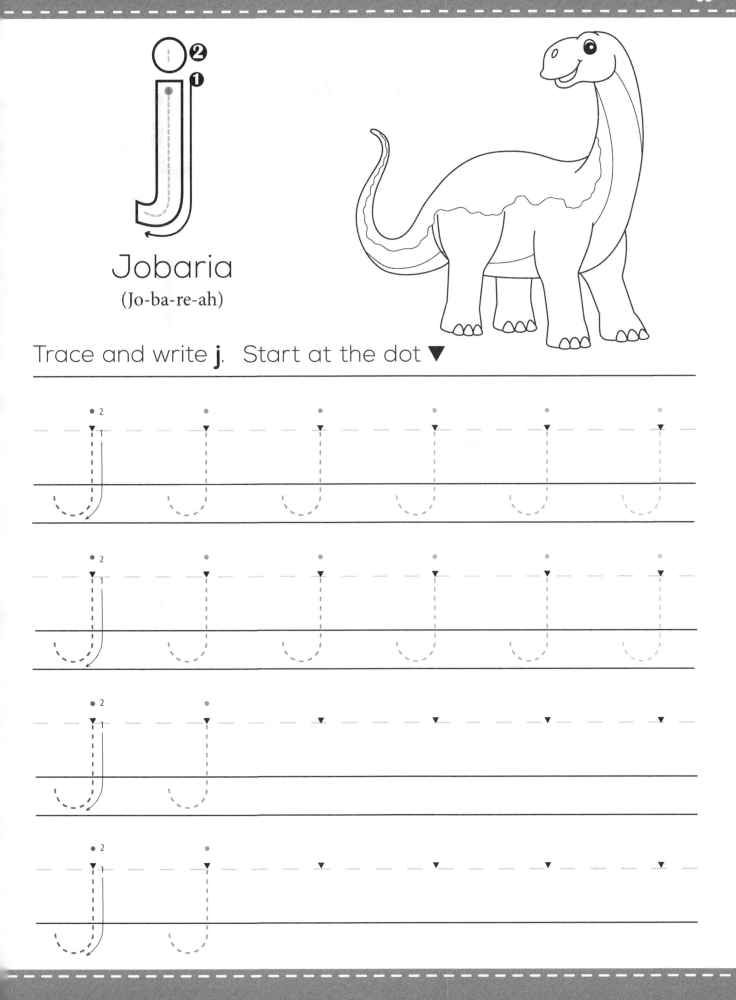

Find the circles with the uppercase letter **J** and color them **green**. Find lowercase letter **j** and color them **pink**.

Jj

- D
- J
- j
- X
- B
- J
- O
- P
- j
- I
- L
- G
- Y
- j
- H
- J
- C

COLOR ME

PUZZLE

Can you help me with each pattern? Write the letter in the empty box that's next to the image that continues the pattern.

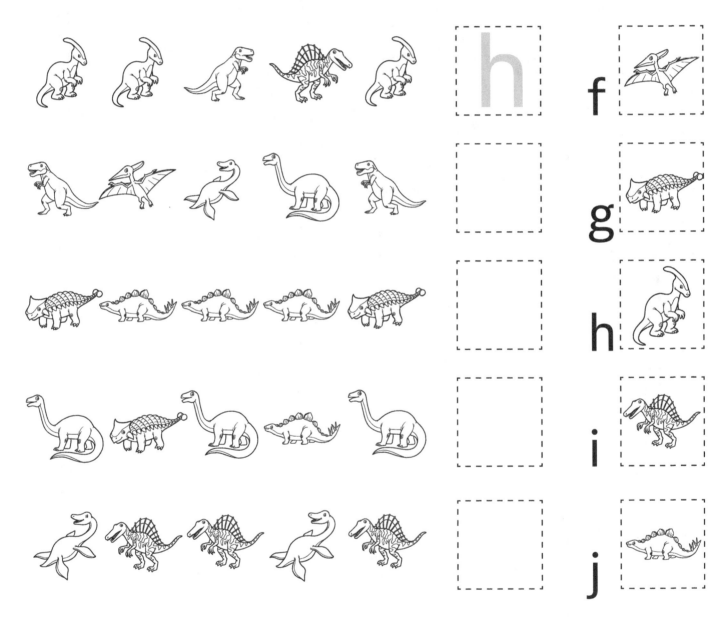

PUZZLE

These dinosaurs are going on an adventure! Can you help them by tracing the lines?

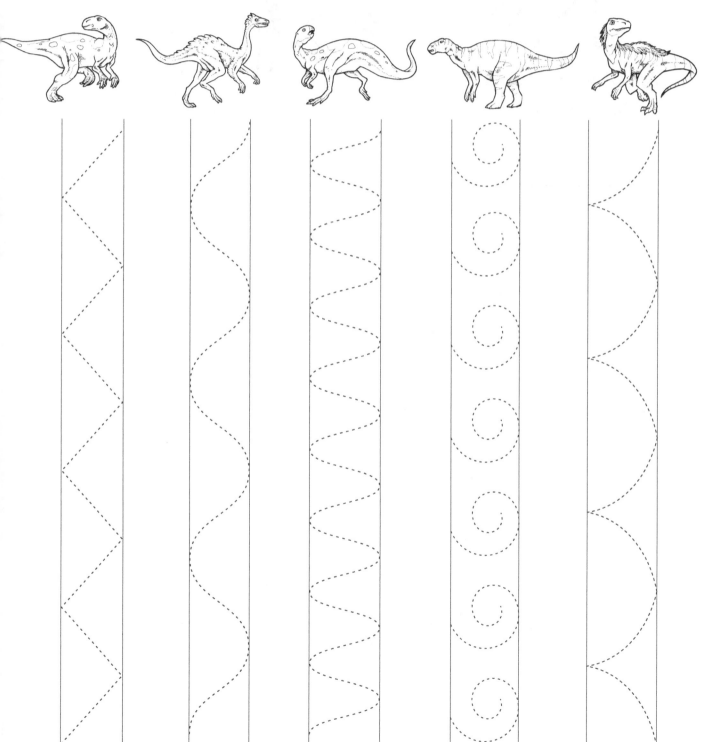

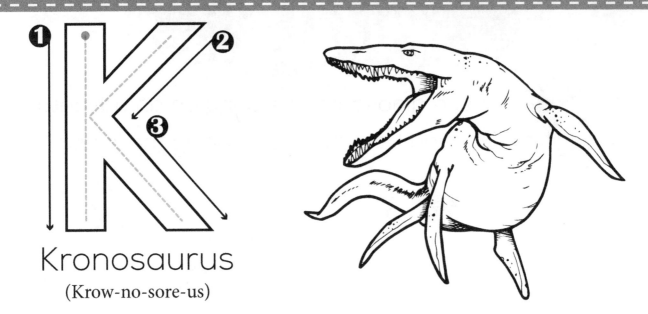

Kronosaurus
(Krow-no-sore-us)

Trace and write **K**. Start at the dot ●

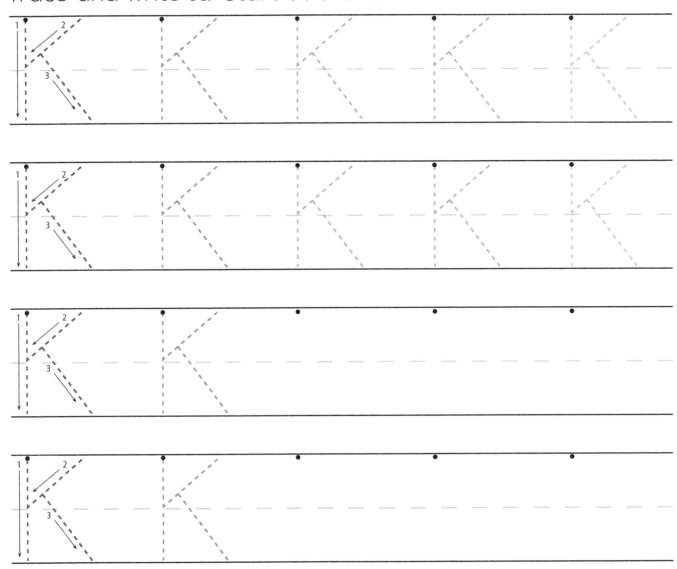

Kentrosaurus

(Ken-tro-saw-rus)

Trace and write **k**. Start at the dot ●

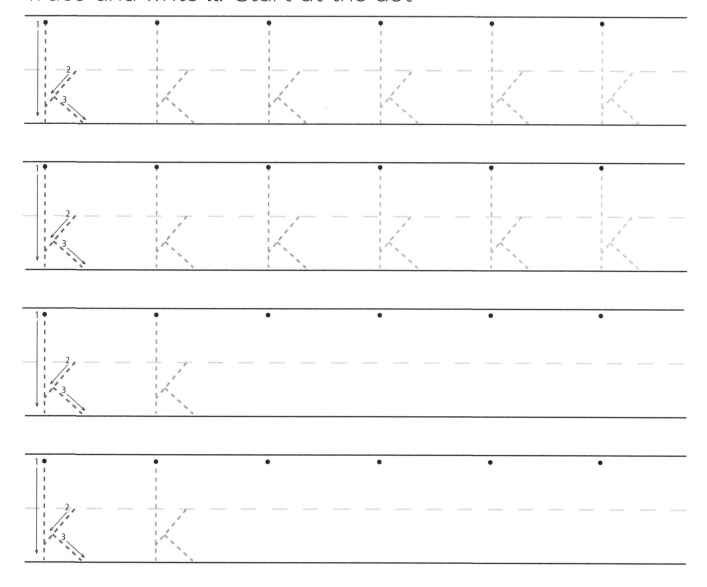

Find the circles with the uppercase letter **K** and color them **black**. Find lowercase letter **k** and color them **cyan**.

Kk

PUZZLE

Jo and Kent want to play together, but first they need to find each other! Can you help?

Start →

Finish

Liaoxiornis
(Lee-ow-i-or-nis)

Trace and write **L**. Start at the dot ●

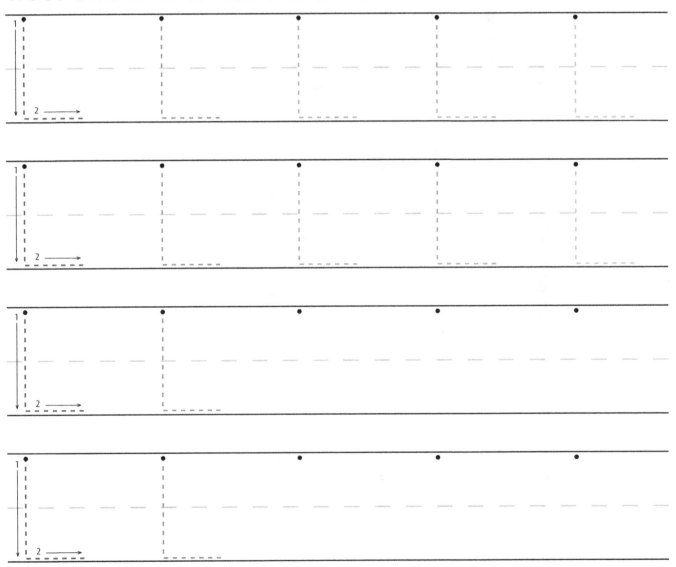

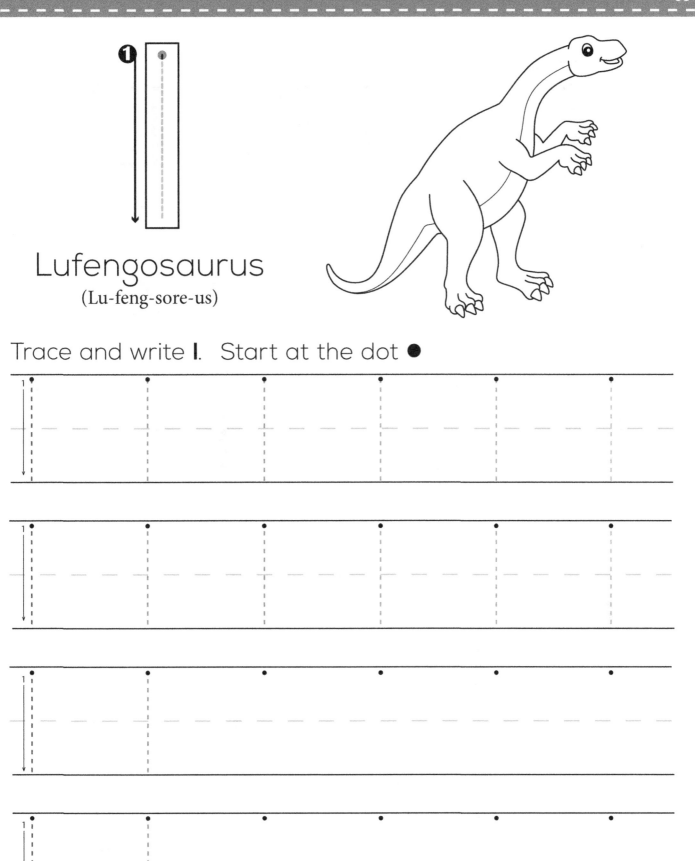

Lufengosaurus
(Lu-feng-sore-us)

Trace and write l. Start at the dot ●

Find the circles with the uppercase letter **L** and color them **grey**. Find lowercase letter **l** and color them **red**.

Ll

E L k
Y c i l
L l l
   l
   L l
   L
I D
   v B

COLOR ME

The dinosaur eggs got all mixed up! Can you help Lu find all of her eggs by coloring all of the L eggs blue?

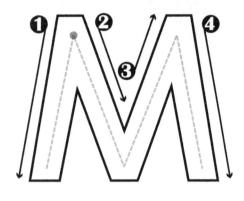

Mosasaurus
(Moe-za-sore-us)

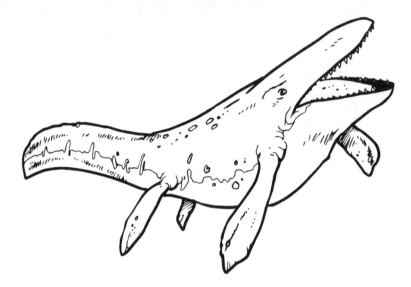

Trace and write **M**. Start at the dot ●

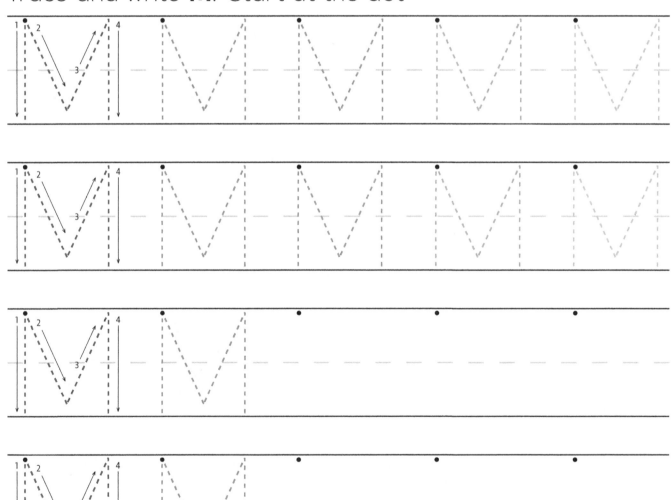

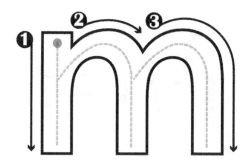

Megalodon
(Meg-ah-low-don)

Trace and write m. Start at the dot ●

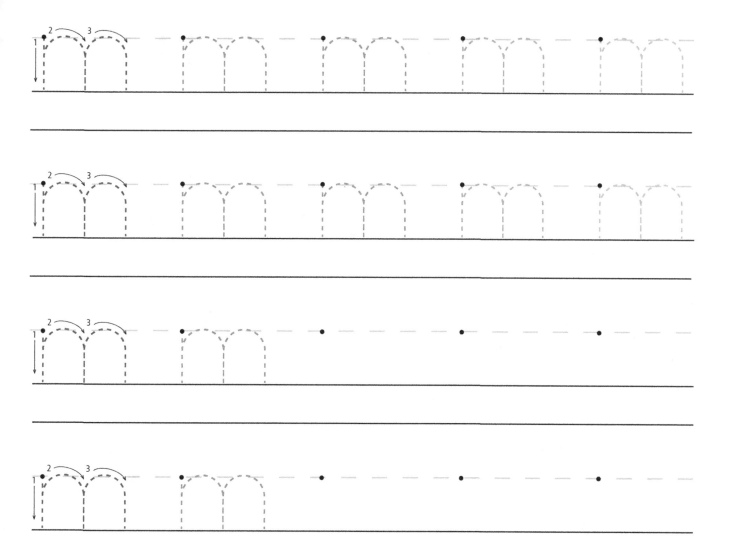

Find the circles with the uppercase letter **M** and color them **orange**. Find lowercase letter **m** and color them **pink**.

Mm

w c k

n M o m

F m m M

Z M P

j L m

PUZZLE

Meg is hungry! Can you help her find all of the letter M's for her to eat? Circle the M's when you find them.

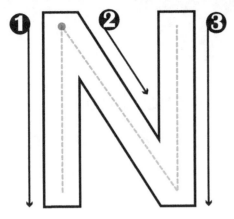

Nothronychus
(Nof-ron-e-kus)

Trace and write **N**. Start at the dot ●

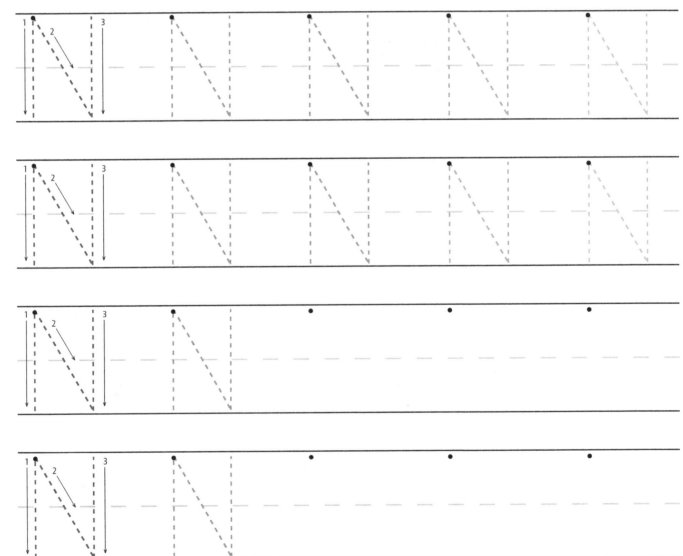

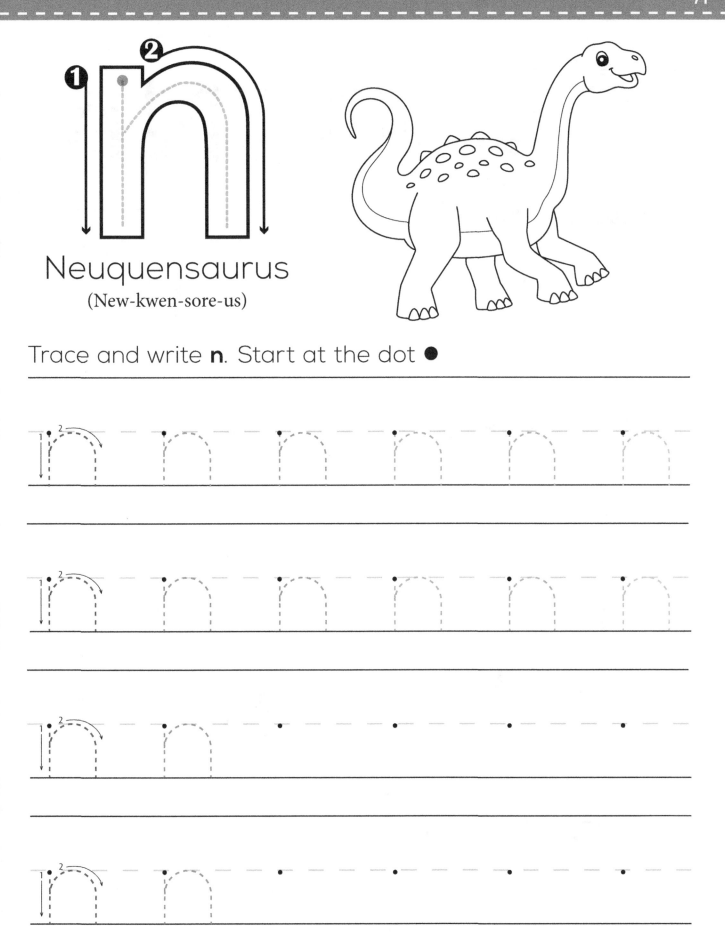

Neuquensaurus
(New-kwen-sore-us)

Trace and write **n**. Start at the dot ●

Find the circles with the uppercase letter **N** and color them **green**. Find lowercase letter **n** and color them **brown**.

Nn

 Quinn is very excited that you'll be drawing a picture of him! He can't wait to see what it looks like.

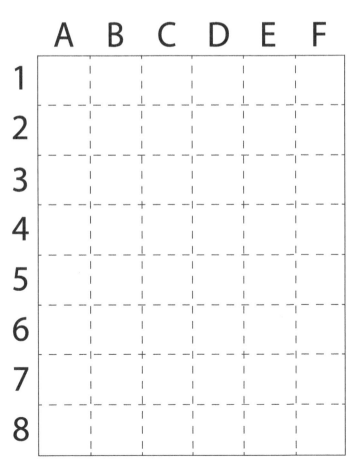

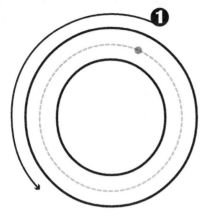

Ouranosaurus
(Or-an-o-sor-us)

Trace and write **O**. Start at the dot ●

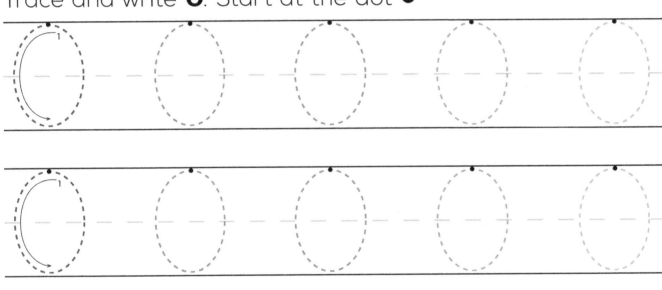
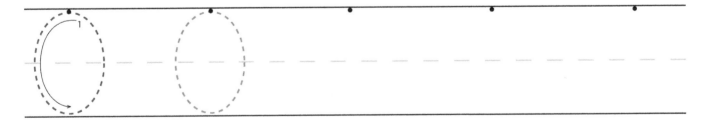
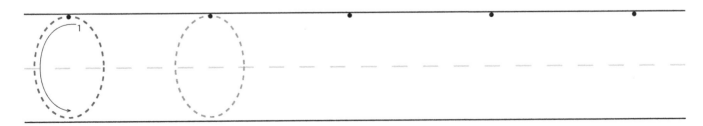

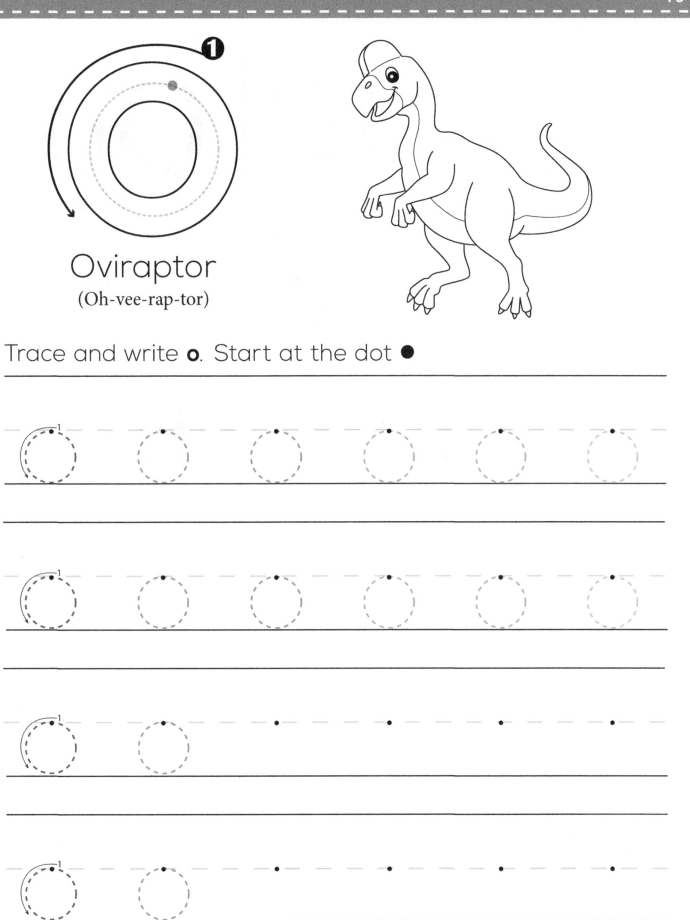

Find the circles with the uppercase letter **O** and color them **yellow**. Find lowercase letter **o** and color them **grey**.

Oo

o O h

v G o D

o m u M

q O o

U L O

PUZZLE

Olivia needs to get back to her eggs. Can you help her find the way?

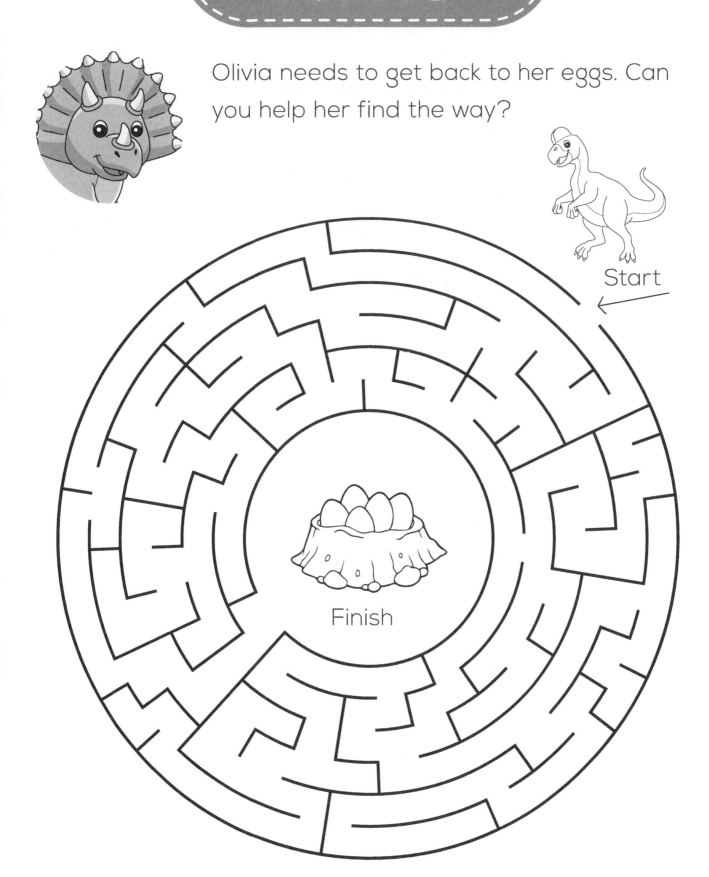

PUZZLE

Can you help me count how many there is of each dinosaur? Write the number on the line below each picture box at the bottom.

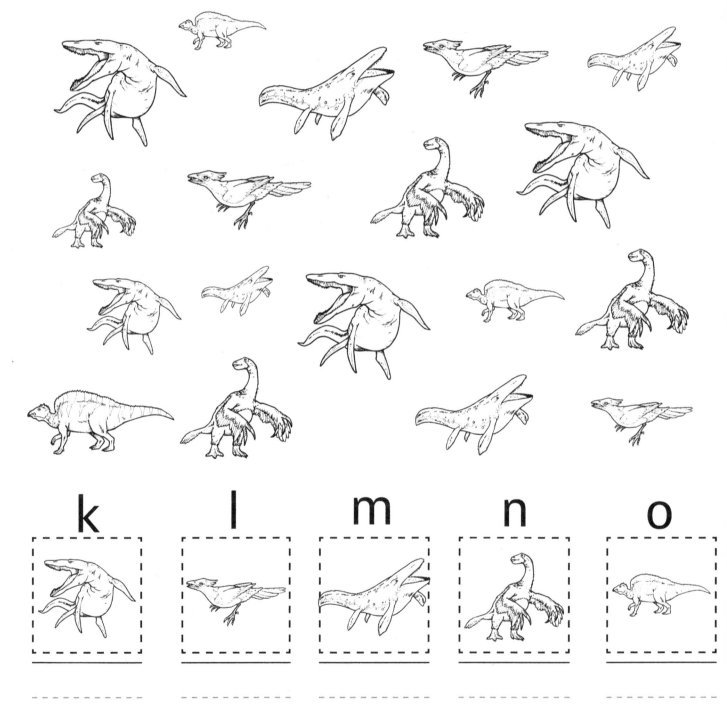

k   l   m   n   o

Oh yay! A word search! Can you find the following words in the word search below?

Egg	Claws	Rocks
Dinosaur	Fossil	Tracks
Bones	Tail	

```
E Z Y Z Z W S J H F
B A Q D T A I L S E
O U J I H W K K R G
N D R N R Z R O G G
E F C O L K V P M C
S Y P S C L A W S R
J F K A R O C K S K
M A C U T N W Y U W
H T X R F O S S I L
T R A C K S J J R R
```

Parasaurolophus
(Pah-rah-sore-o-loe-fus)

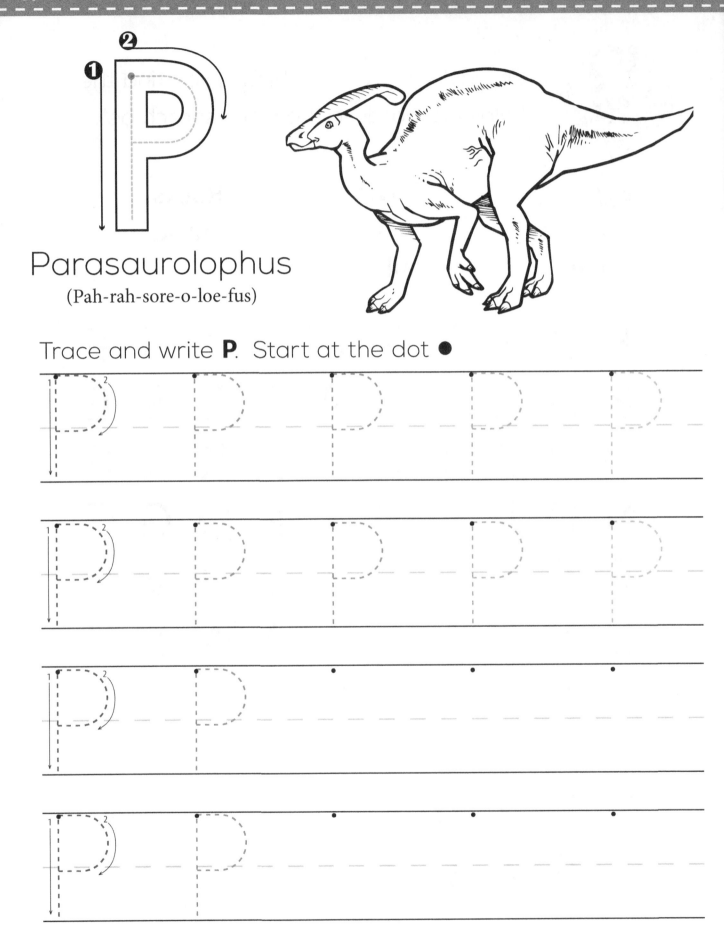

Trace and write P. Start at the dot ●

Pterodon
(Teh-roe-don)

Trace and write **p**. Start at the dot ●

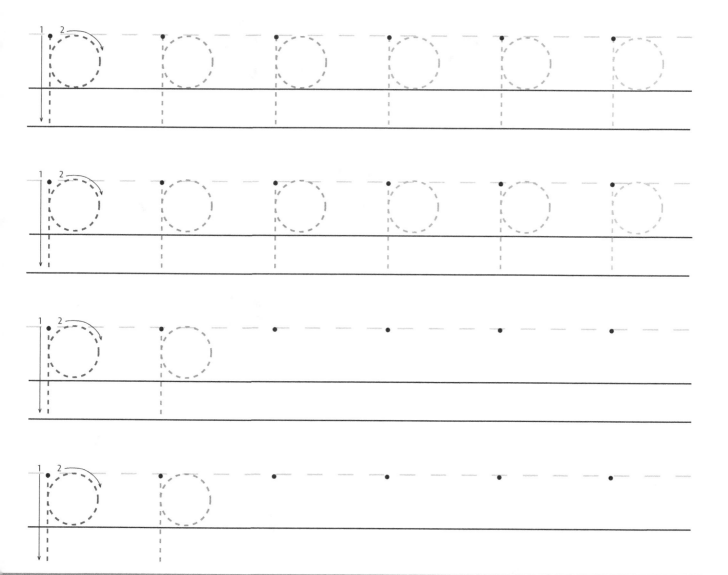

Find the circles with the uppercase letter **P** and color them **purple**. Find lowercase letter **p** and color them **blue**.

Pp

P   y   k

R   p   P   p

S   d   b

p   P   u

o   D   p   B

PUZZLE

Oh no! The dinosaurs lost their shadows! Let's help them find the right ones. Draw a line from the left to the right when you find a match.

Draw lines to match the letter pairs.

I J K L

k i l j

M N O P

n p m o

 Let's do a quick review! Trace the letters below and say the sound each one makes.

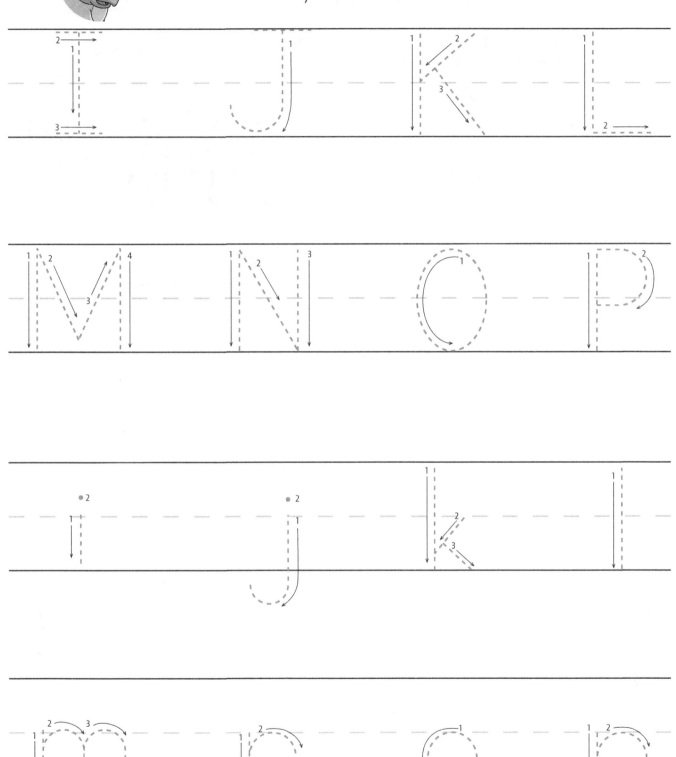

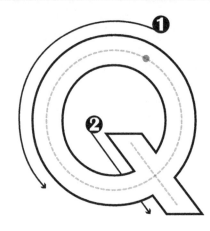

Quaesitosaurus
(Kway-sit-oh-sore-us)

Trace and write **Q**. Start at the dot ●

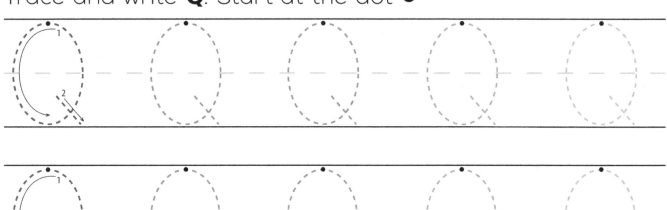

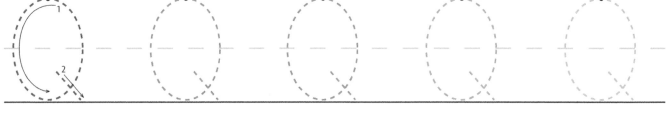

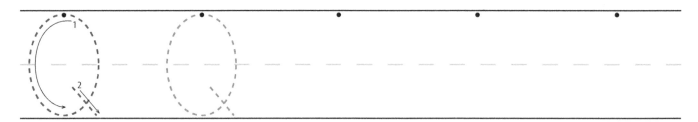

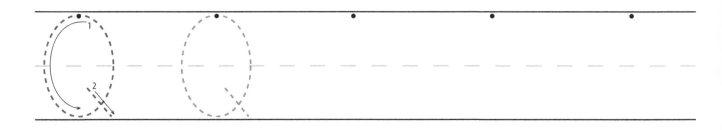

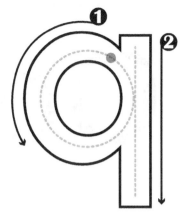

Qantassaurus
(Kwan-tass-sore-us)

Trace and write q. Start at the dot ●

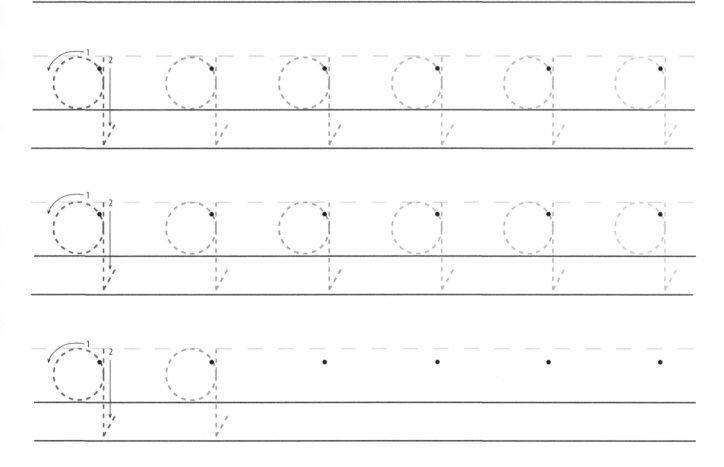

Find the circles with the uppercase letter **Q** and color them **black**. Find lowercase letter **q** and color them **cyan**.

Qq

COLOR ME

Rebbachisaurus
(Reb-bok-e-sore-us)

Trace and write **R**. Start at the dot ●

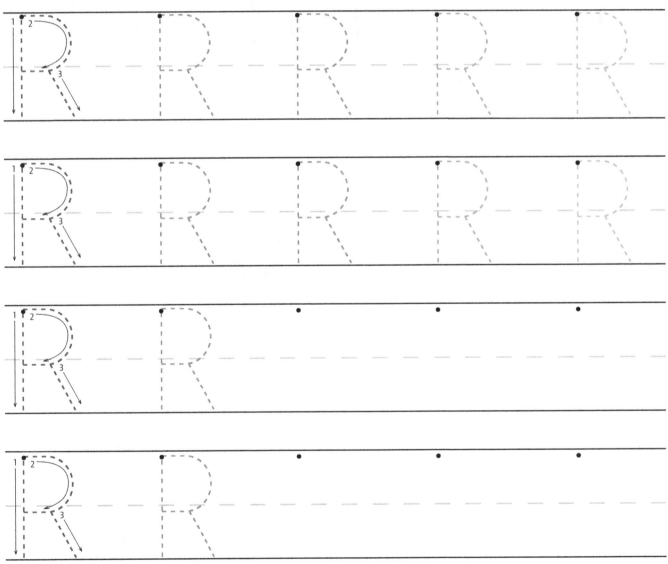

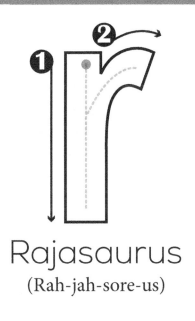

Rajasaurus
(Rah-jah-sore-us)

Trace and write **r**. Start at the dot ●

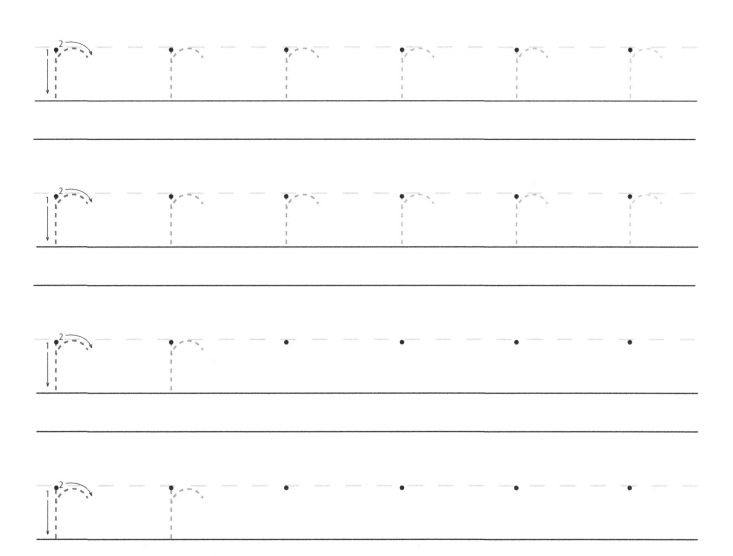

Find the circles with the uppercase letter **R** and color them **red**. Find lowercase letter **r** and color them **brown**.

R r

R z l
r p n r
q R b
 r P u
r R r a

Let's do a puzzle!

Find your way from the **start** to the **finsh**, following the lowercase letter **r**.

Start

Finish

Stegosaurus
(Steg-oh-sore-us)

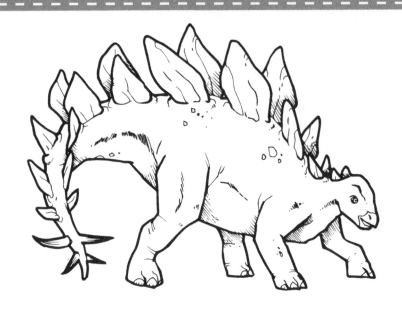

Trace and write **S**. Start at the dot ●

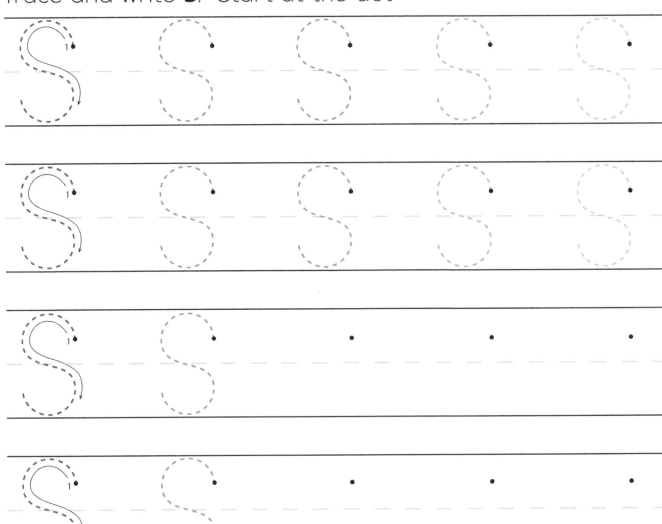

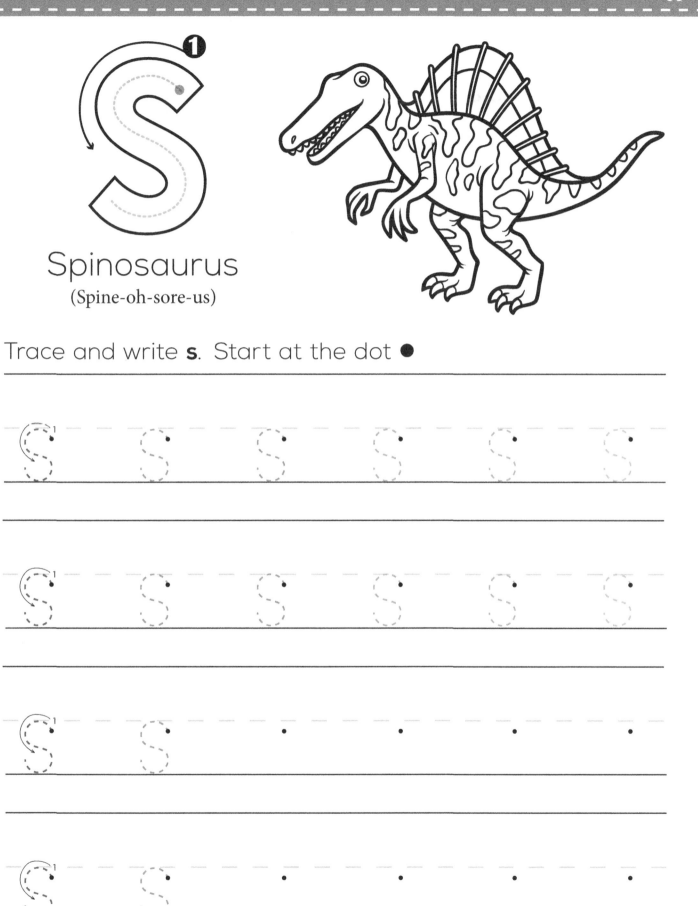

Spinosaurus
(Spine-oh-sore-us)

Trace and write **s**. Start at the dot ●

Find the circles with the uppercase letter **S** and color them **cyan**. Find lowercase letter **s** and color them **orange**.

Ss

PUZZLE

Steve needs some help! It looks like we need to complete the dots from A-S to help him out.

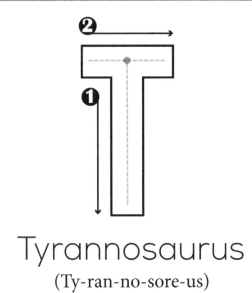

Tyrannosaurus
(Ty-ran-no-sore-us)

Trace and write **T**. Start at the dot ●

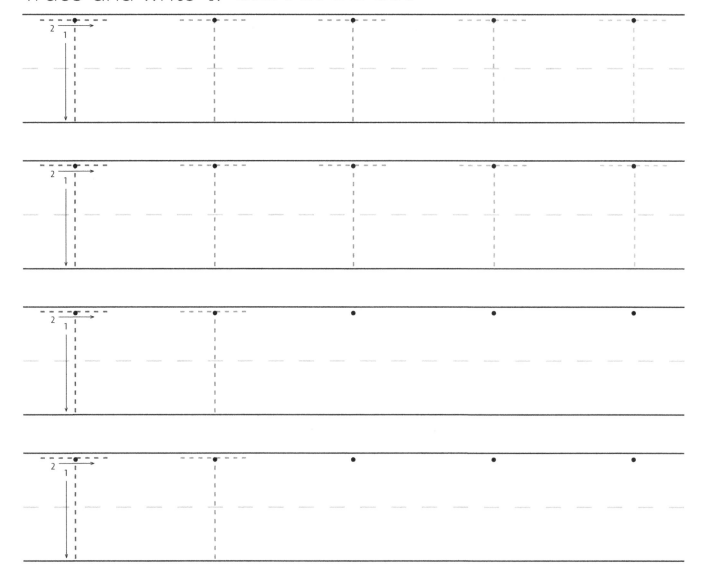

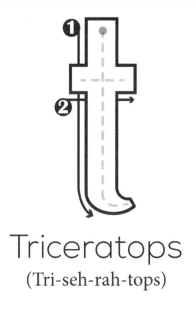

Triceratops
(Tri-seh-rah-tops)

Trace and write **t**. Start at the dot ●

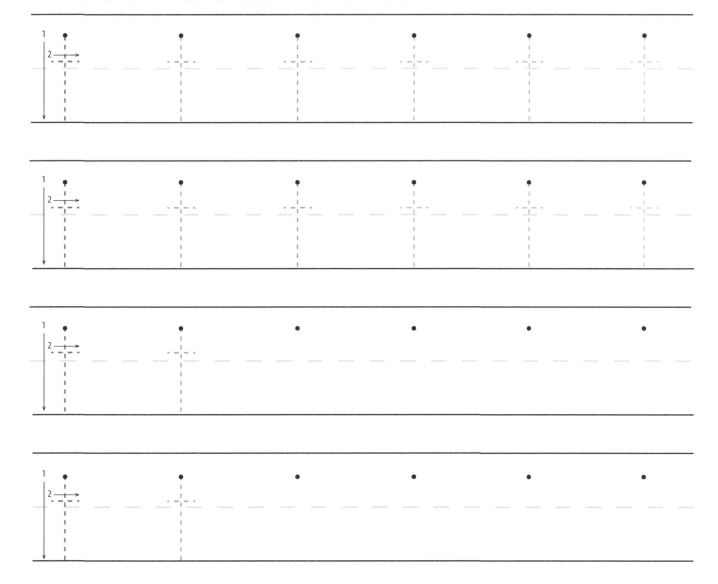

Find the circles with the uppercase letter **T** and color them **grey**. Find lowercase letter **t** and color them **yellow**.

Tt

Oh! Look! You get to draw me! I bet it will turn out fabulous!

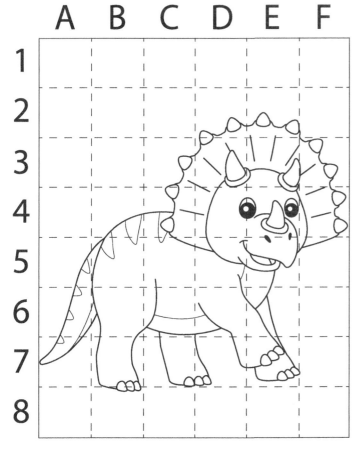

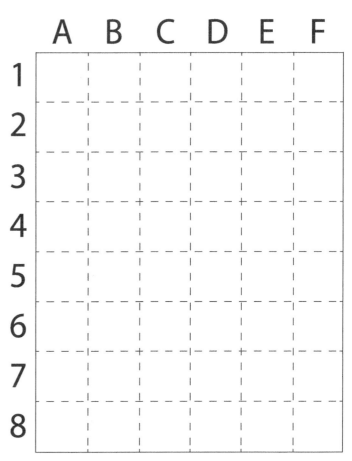

COLOR ME

My friend Rex would love to be colored. Can you help him?

Q: Light brown
R: Dark brown
S: Tan
T: Grey (Claws)

COLOR ME

Urbacodon
(Ur-bak-o-don)

Trace and write **U**. Start at the dot ●

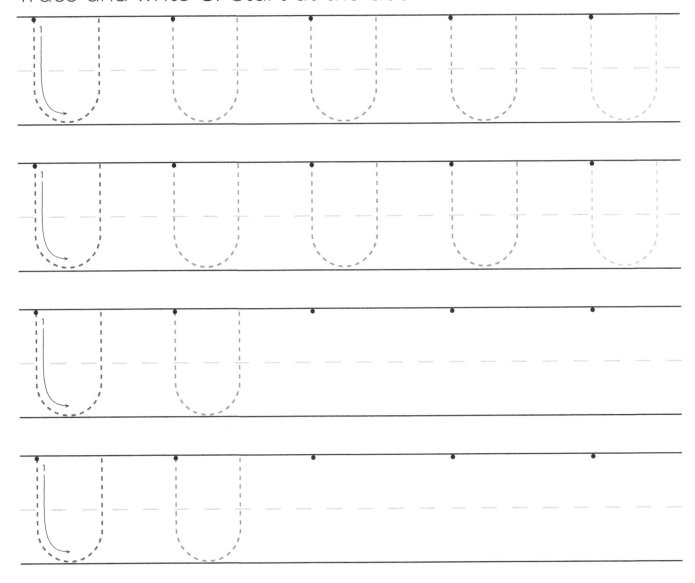

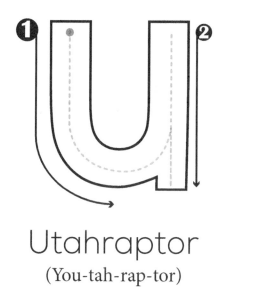

Utahraptor
(You-tah-rap-tor)

Trace and write **u**. Start at the dot ●

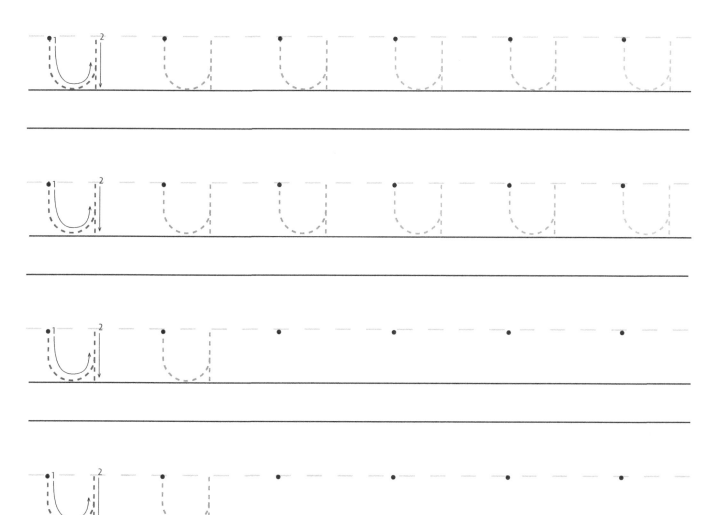

Find the circles with the uppercase letter **U** and color them **pink**. Find lowercase letter **u** and color them **blue**.

Uu

PUZZLE

Utah is hungry! Can you help him find all of the letter U's for him to eat? Circle the U's when you find them.

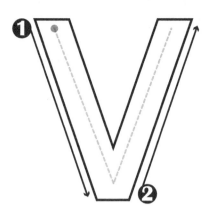

Velociraptor
(Vell-oss-e-rap-tor)

Trace and write **V**. Start at the dot ●

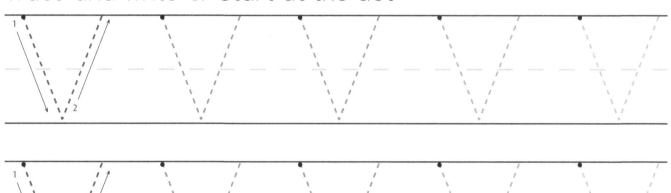

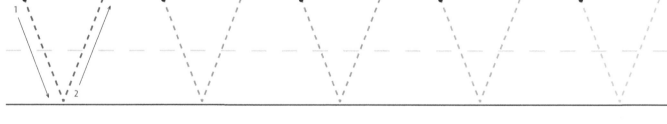

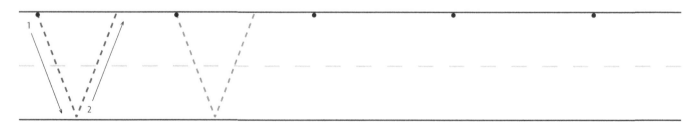

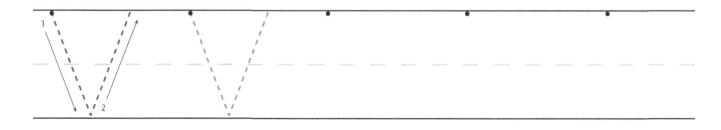

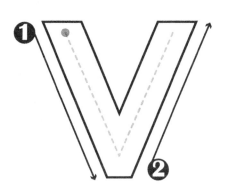

Viavenator
(Vy-ah-ven-ah-tor)

Trace and write **v**. Start at the dot ●

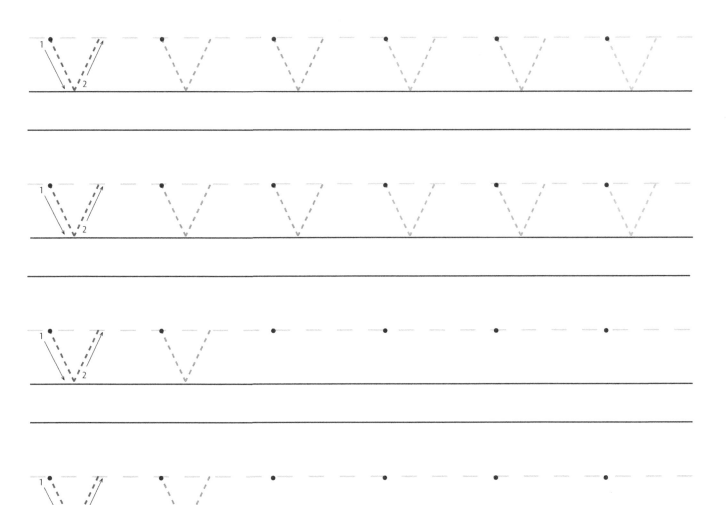

Find the circles with the uppercase letter **V** and color them **black**. Find lowercase letter **v** and color them **green**.

Vv

PUZZLE

Velma needs some help! It looks like we need to complete the dots from A-V to help her out.

Draw lines to match the letter pairs.

Q R S

s q r

T U V

u t v

 Let's do a quick review! Trace the letters below and say the sound each one makes.

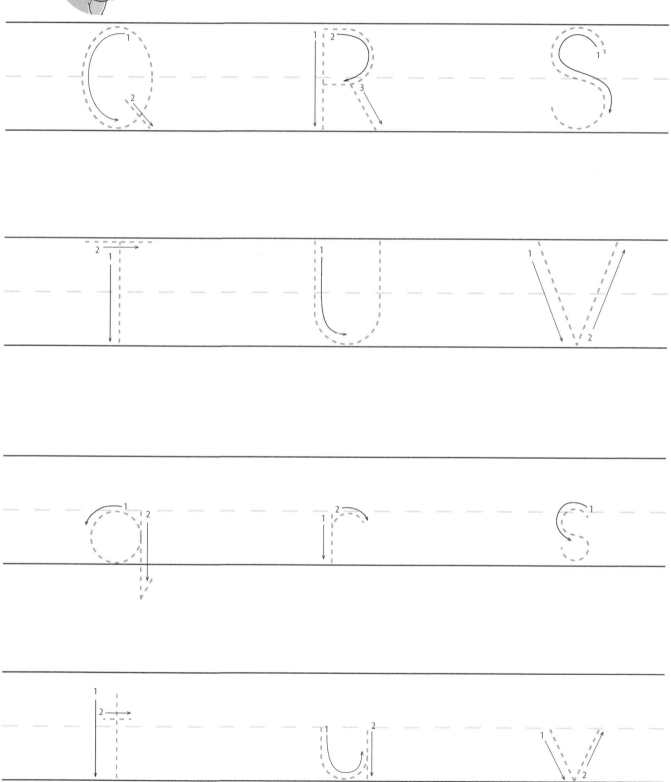

Wuerhosaurus
(Where-ho-sore-us)

Trace and write **W**. Start at the dot ●

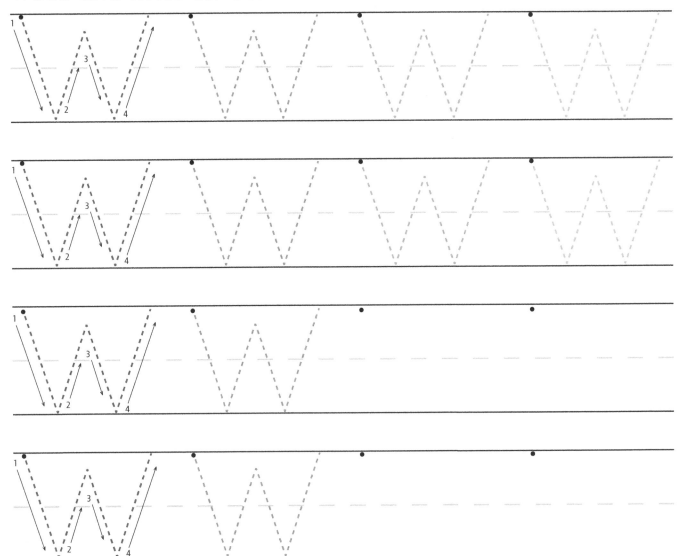

Wannanosaurus
(Wan-nan-oh-sore-us)

Trace and write **w**. Start at the dot ●

Find the circles with the uppercase letter **W** and color them **yellow**. Find lowercase letter **w** and color them **brown**.

Ww

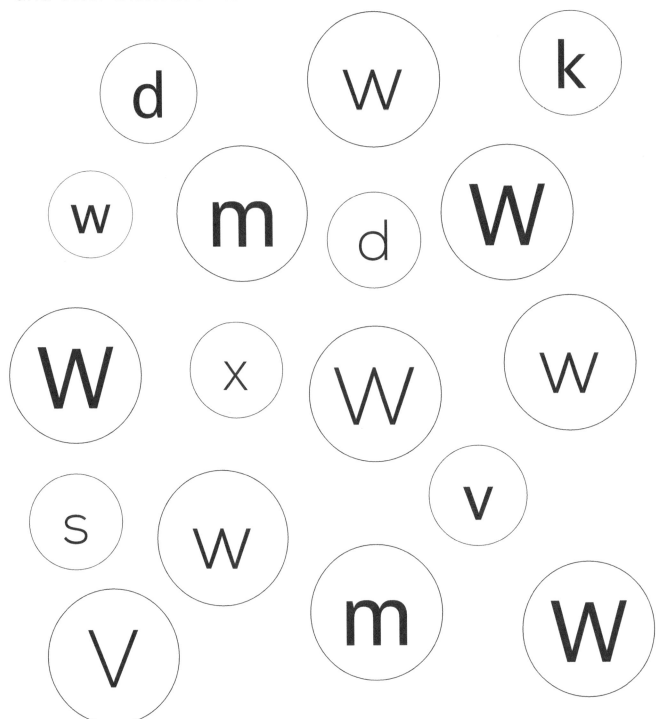

COLOR ME

Xenotarsosaurus
(Zee-noe-tar-so-sore-us)

Trace and write **X**. Start at the dot ●

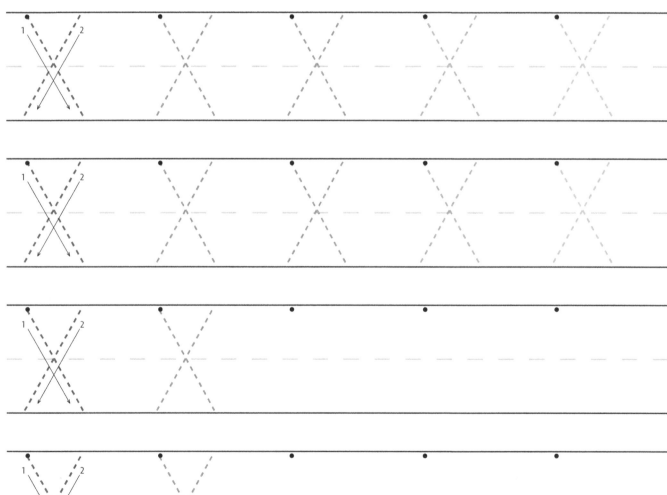

Xenoceratops
(Zee-noe-seh-rah-tops)

Trace and write **x**. Start at the dot ●

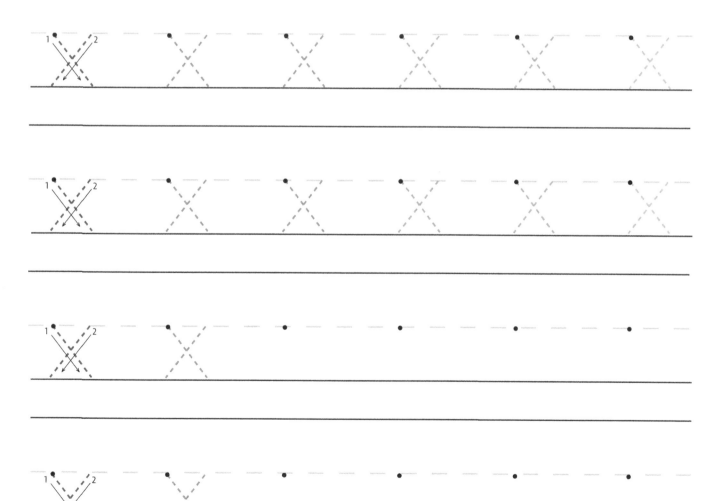

Find the circles with the uppercase letter **X** and color them **black**. Find lowercase letter **x** and color them **purple**.

PUZZLE

Xeno needs to get back to her eggs. Can you help her through the maze?

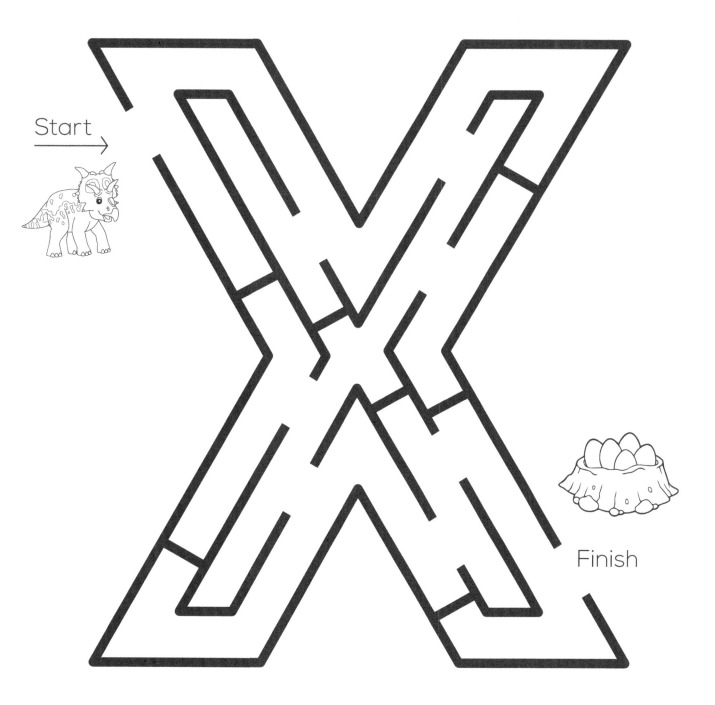

Start

Finish

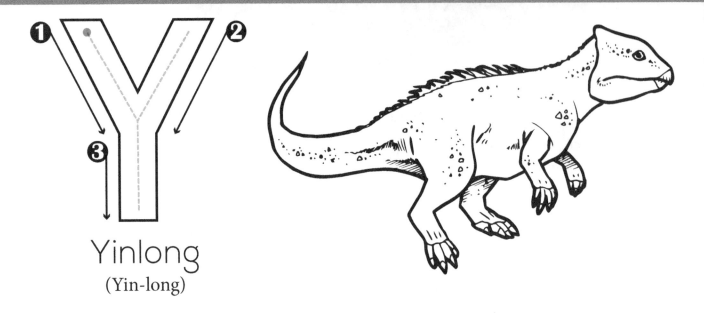

Yinlong
(Yin-long)

Trace and write **Y**. Start at the dot ●

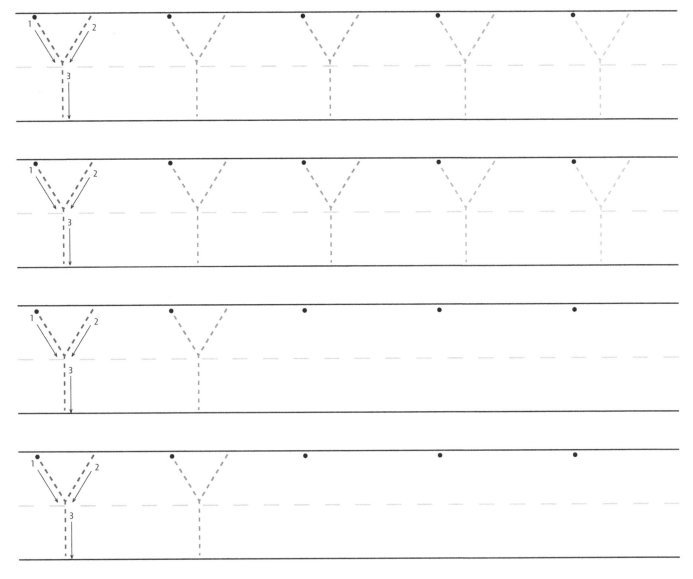

Yangchuanosaurus
(Yang-chwan-oh-sore-us)

Trace and write **y**. Start at the dot ●

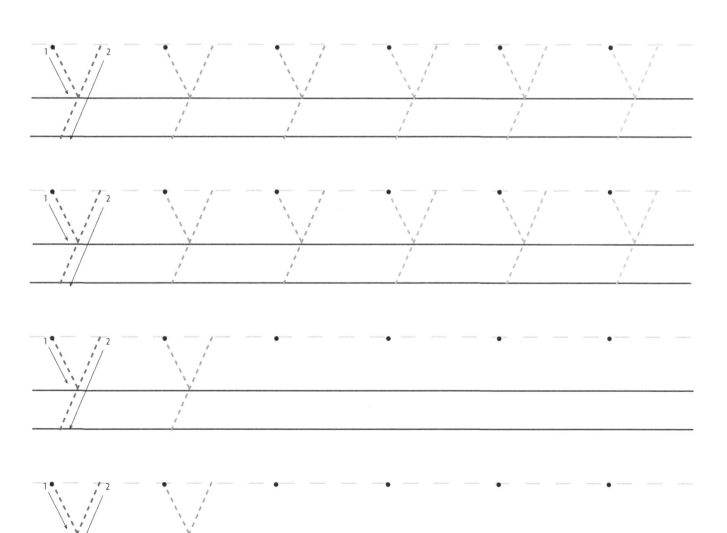

Find the circles with the uppercase letter **Y** and color them **grey**. Find lowercase letter **y** and color them **cyan**.

Yy

COLOR ME

The dinosaur eggs got all mixed up! Can you help Yang find all of her eggs by coloring all of the Y eggs Yellow?

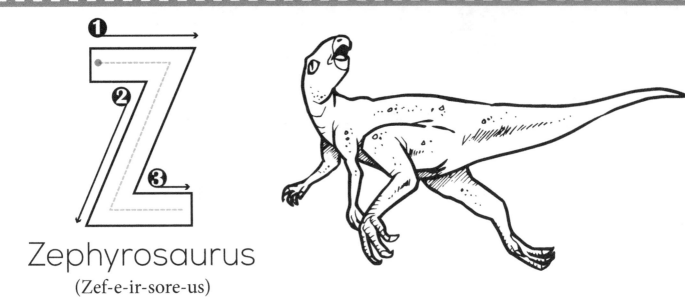

Zephyrosaurus
(Zef-e-ir-sore-us)

Trace and write **Z**. Start at the dot ●

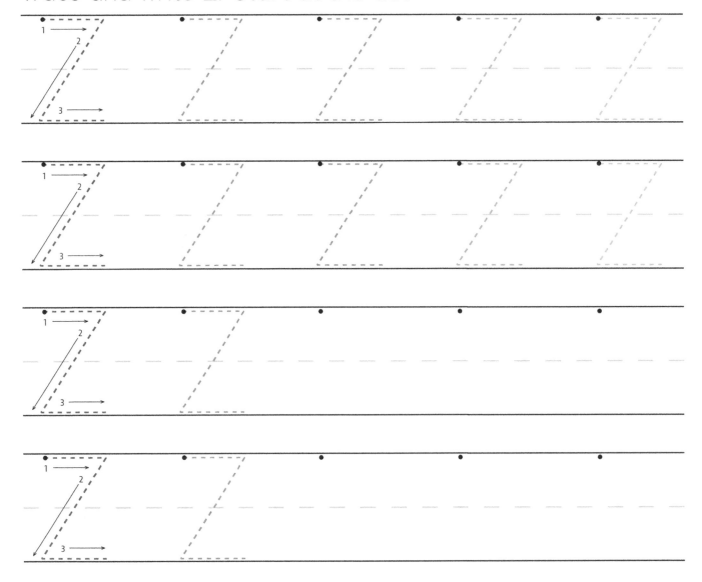

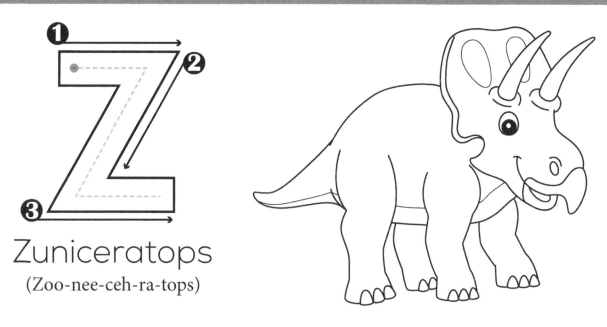

Zuniceratops
(Zoo-nee-ceh-ra-tops)

Trace and write **z**. Start at the dot •

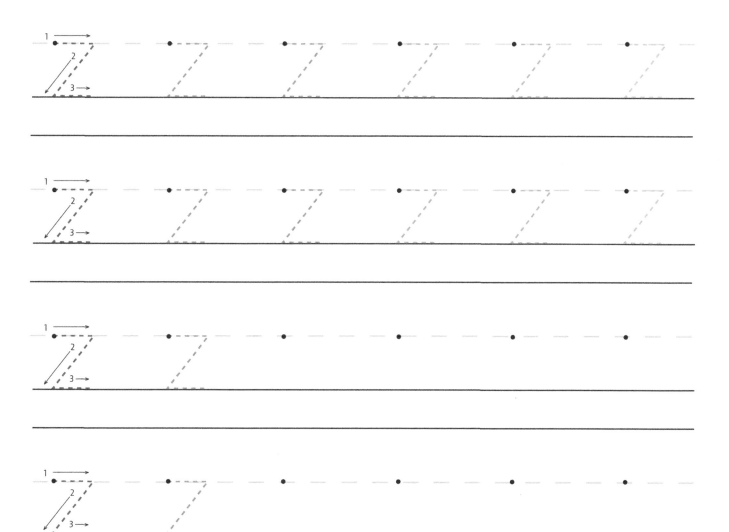

Find the circles with the uppercase letter **Z** and color them **red**. Find lowercase letter **z** and color them **green**.

Zz

Oh yay! A word search! Can you find the following dinosaur names in the word search below?

Zuniceratops
Zephyrosaurus
Velociraptor
Triceratops

Stegosaurus
Pterodon
Jobaria
Iguanodon

Diplodocus
Carnotaurus
Apatosaurus

```
P S A O I Z J D V H R T V V Y
Z U L T L E O O E G S K D A L
E G Z R F P B K L S C X I U Q
U E U I W H A P O T A X P P B
Z O N C K Y R A C E R U L T S
B O I E V R I K I G N R O E I
R P C R T O A Y R O O K D R G
I K E A M S B F A S T R O O U
T U R T M A U H P A A S C D A
T E A O A U A C T U U G U O N
O L T P X R H I O R R O S N O
I O O S V U Q I R U U Q Q B D
S P P A H S F V C S S J F H O
C C S A P A T O S A U R U S N
O L R N X O A B O W F G D K K
```

Draw lines to match the letter pairs.

W

X

X

z

Y

W

Z

y

Let's do a quick review! Trace the letters below and say the sound each one makes.

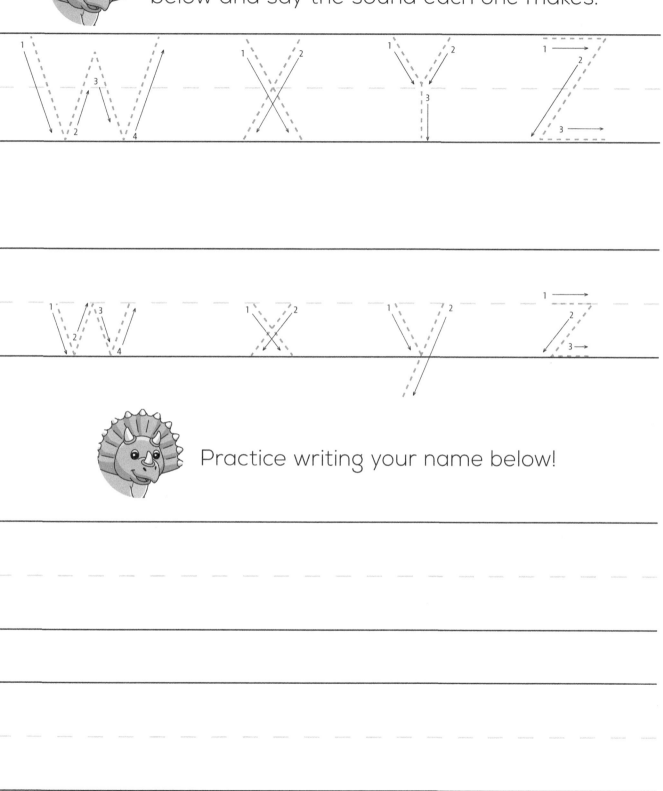

Practice writing your name below!

PUZZLE

We did it! We are almost to the very end of our adventure! Just for fun, can you complete the following dinosaur going from A-Z?

COLOR ME

Trace the letters. Say the names and sounds of each letter.

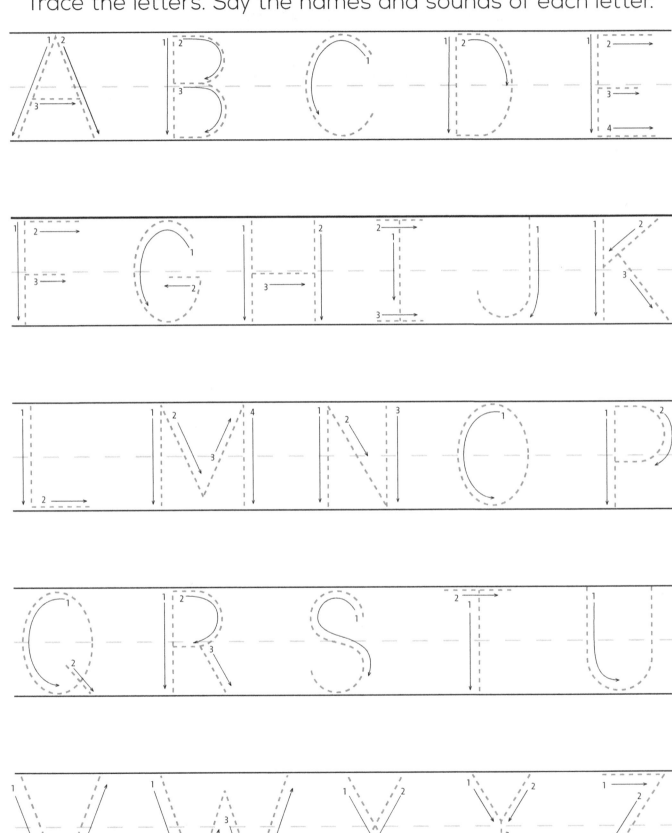

Trace the letters. Say the names and sounds of each letter.

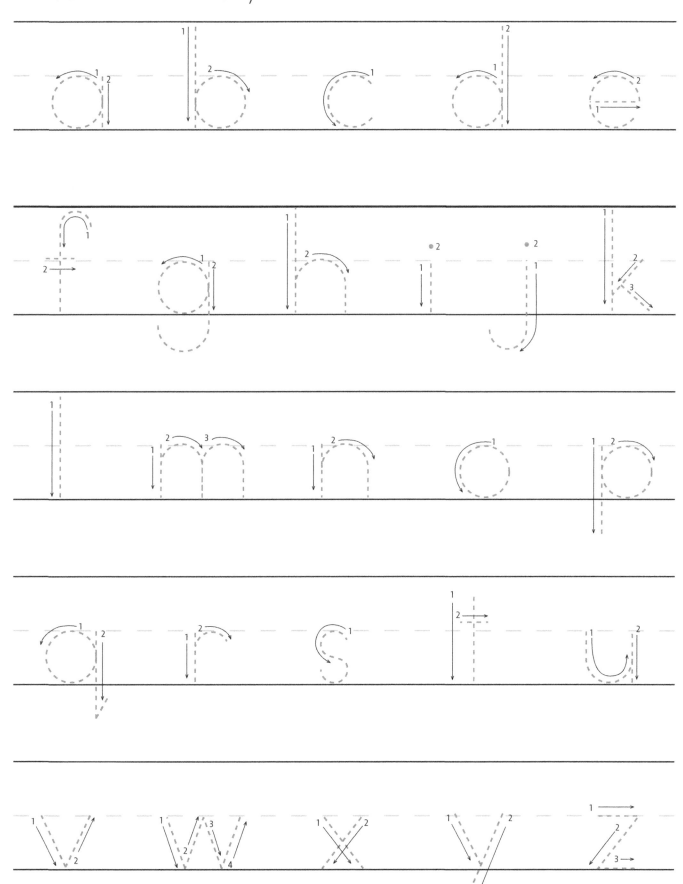

Use the lines to practice letters, writing your name, or anything you'd like!

Use the lines to practice letters, writing your name, or anything you'd like!

Use the lines to practice letters, writing your name, or anything you'd like!

Thank you so much for helping me on our adventure! I learned so much!

You did amazing! I hope you had fun meeting all of my friends!

Which activity was your favorite?

Which dinosaur was your favorite?

Did you enjoy this book?
Please leave a review.

Visit us online at
www.ScribbleKidsPress.com

Email: scribblekidspress@gmail.com

Made in the USA
Las Vegas, NV
13 July 2024